BOOKS BY RICHARD WORMSER

SOUTHWEST COOKERY OR AT HOME ON THE RANGE

THE YELLOWLEGS

RIDE A NORTHBOUND HORSE

THE KIDNAPPED CIRCUS

THE LONESOME QUARTER

SOUTHWEST
COOKERY or
At Home on the Range

For Nancy & Jerry,
   This may literally make you
home sick. (At least you'll
enjoy the reading.)
   We miss you already.
   Happy Christmas 2006
   With love,
      Judy & Ed

Southwest
Cookery

OR

AT HOME ON THE RANGE

Richard Wormser

ILLUSTRATED BY PAT RONSON STEWART

TABLE OF CONTENTS

1 FIRST THINGS FIRST   1

Dips, Seafood Cocktails and two Tequila Drinks.

2 SOUP ALL DAY LONG   11

Clear and Thick Soups, and the Special Dry Soups from Mexico.

3 SALADS, BOTH WILD AND TAME   25

Herb Salads, some from more conventional greens, Bean Salads, and a couple of Avocado recipes.

4 A FEW PIQUANT SAUCES   37

How to make your own Chile Sauces, both table and kitchen types. Hints on buying chile.

5 TO REFRY OR NOT?   45

The Beans that are the very heart of Southwestern cooking; Different Varieties; the Chick-pea.

6 THE ALMOST MYSTICAL EGG   59

The great things done to it by Mexicans, Spanish, and other Southwesterners.

7 NOT ALL THE COUNTRY IS DRY   67

Fish recipes, both Freshwater and Salt.

8 LIFE STARTS WITH CORN 83

Tacos, Tamales, Enchiladas, Tamale Pie, and other basic dishes.

9 MEAT MAKES THE CARNIVAL 99

Kid, Lamb, Mutton, Beef, and Pork.

10 YARDBIRDS 125

Domestic Poultry, mostly Chicken and Turkey.

11 AVOID THE JACKRABBIT 137

Cooking Game at home and in the field.

12 HOMEGROWN 149

Dried and Fresh Vegetables.

13 THE SWEET LAND! 157

Southwestern Desserts, and a few from Mexico proper.

INDEX 169

Recipes whose titles are capitalized may be found by consulting the Index.

AUTHOR'S NOTE

Unless otherwise noted, as in some of the egg dishes, all recipes are for four people. Salt is omitted from most recipes as the amount is a matter of personal taste; but for cooks unfamiliar with chile cooking, it should be pointed out that the spice seems to absorb and counteract salt; use more salt than you are accustomed to.

INTRODUCTION

We eat well in the Southwest. In fact, we think we eat better than anybody anywhere else, which probably isn't true, but it makes us feel good.

By Southwest, this book means Arizona and New Mexico; several other areas, such as Texas and Oklahoma, lay claim to the title.

Of course, our cooking is influenced by our neighbors to the south, the states of Chihuahua and Sonora in Mexico. These are the hot-cooking states of Old Mexico; in Mexico City very hot dishes are called northern plates, *platillos nortenses.*

But the Americans of Mexican descent who make up a large part of the population of the southern tier of the Southwest are not all oriented to Senora and Chihuahua. They came from all over the Republic, in large numbers, during the years when the last Mexican Revolution was petering out, over fifty years ago, and they brought their family recipes with them.

Central Mexico contributed a strong French influence, from the occupation of the country by troops of Napoleon III supporting the short, sad rule of Maximilian and Carlota.

More French influence came from New Orleans, across Texas, and from Taos, where French-Canadian trappers used to winter.

Presently, many of our fresh vegetables come from California—the rest are from the lower Rio Grande Valley in Texas—and salads are widely eaten. The old-time cowboy would have scorned them, but nowadays—since World War II, really—no ranch can keep riders if the mess hall doesn't put a good salad on the table.

Germans entered the Southwest in two waves. When the Santa Fe Trail opened up, after Mexico threw off Spanish rule, German traders flocked to New Mexico, some of them from St. Louis and others directly from Prussia. Then, in the Mexican Revolution, a number of Germans who didn't want to fight for the Kaiser enlisted with Pancho Villa, and while most of them settled in Mexico after the Revolution, several chose to settle north of the border.

They are almost all gone now, but when I first moved around the Southwest, thirty years ago, I met several German Villistas.

The influence of the old Fred Harvey chain of depot-lunchrooms should not be minimized. There are still a few Harvey restaurants operating, such as at the Grand Canyon, and Santa Fe and Albuquerque, and the company still caters on the Santa Fe Railroad; but Fred Harvey's influence went farther afield than that: ex-cooks and Harvey girls—waitresses—married, quit their jobs, and opened their own restaurants, using Fred Harvey recipes.

So our cooking is not all hot and peppery. Quite the contrary.

But in the northern tier of counties, especially in New Mexico, chile is used and highly prized. Someone once said that it was in the upper Rio Grande Valley that the heavenly marriage between the tomato and the chile was made.

Rio Grande chile is different from that grown in Mexico, but very similar to that from the Santa Cruz Valley in southern Arizona, and, for that matter, to the coastal chile grown around Oxnard, California. It does not in any way except fierceness resemble cayenne.

Nor is it very closely related to chili powder, which is a Texas concoction and can be very good. But to get the real chile flavor through from chili powder—which contains other herbs and spices, dried garlic, and so on—so much has to be used that the food becomes much too hot.

Good chile helps you digest your food, fills you with vitamins, and leaves a wonderful aftertaste.

There are plenty of chile recipes in this book.

There are also plenty of recipes for dishes made with tortillas, mostly the corn tortilla that is made of stone-ground hominy and carries with it a faint taste of lava dust and lye.

Here Texas comes to the rescue: El Paso and San Antonio tortillas, canned in a vacuum tin, are available all over the United States.

So is canned green chile. Ground, dried red chile may be more of a problem, but there are New Mexico companies that will send it out mail order. The Santa Cruz Chile & Spice Co., Tumacacori, Arizona 85640 is reliable. All the other spices and herbs used in the Southwest are available elsewhere.

There are recipes for every taste here, mild ones, moderate ones, rather hot ones.

Have a good time; try them all.

SOUTHWEST
COOKERY or
At Home on the Range

First things first

APPETIZERS AND COCKTAILS

In old-world Spanish, hors d'oeuvres are called *entremeses*. I've seen and heard them called *antecomidas*, before-meals, along the border and in Arizona. In Mexico, particularly northern New Mexico, they are sometimes called *meriendas*, which properly should be reserved for meals-between-meals, which the English call Elevenses, or for afternoon tea.

Olives, drained of their brine and allowed to marinate in lemon juice obviously migrated from Spain, but the little, very hot, acorn-shaped *jalapeño* peppers, pickled and sometimes stuffed with anchovies, are very Mexican. Salted piñon nuts are New Mexican, and Guacamole is a semi-tropical dish.

My wife makes the best Guacamole in the world, a point not open to argument. Our Spanish neighbors, when they give a party, always call on her to furnish the green dip, and Mexican bachelors, after tasting it, have been known to eye me in what I could only construe as a sinister manner.

There are hundreds of other recipes for Guacamole. You don't need them.

GUACAMOLE
(*Avocado Dip*)

2 small, ripe avocados	1 freshly hard-cooked egg
1 small onion, grated	⅓ stick (⅙ cup) butter
1 four-ounce can chopped green chiles	2 tablespoons mayonnaise

Peel, pit, and mash the avocados. If the Guacamole is not going to be used within an hour or so, reserve the pit. Stir in the grated onion and chopped chiles. In a separate bowl, grate the warm egg over the butter and work in the mayonnaise with a French whisk; gradually add the contents of the other bowl, taste and salt. Putting the avocado pit in the middle of the mixture will keep the Guacamole from turning black in the refrigerator.

The other favorite dip at Southwestern parties is served hot, in a chafing dish or over a warmer. Its name, Chile con Queso, is typically reversed in the Spanish manner; there is more cheese, *queso,* than there is chile, but Spanish-speaking people put the more important ingredient second in many of their food names.

CHILE CON QUESO
(*Cheese and Chile Dip*)

1 small onion, grated	1 four-ounce can green chiles, chopped
¼ pound butter	
1 pound sharp club cheese	1 tablespoon coarse-ground red chile (*chile caribe*)

Cook the grated onion in the butter over low heat until the onion is transparent. Crumble the cheese fairly fine and add it; stir until the cheese begins to melt, then add the green chile slowly, so as not to cool the cheese. Add the red chile and continue stirring until chile is well distributed. Serve warm.

The third most popular dip is never served if the dinner that follows has beans on the menu, as it almost always does in the southern tier of the Southwest, and often in the northern counties as well. But for a cocktail party, followed by dispersal rather than dinner, all three dips are traditional.

BEAN DIP
(*Pasta de Frijoles*)

2 cups cooked or canned pinto beans in chile sauce	2 tablespoons grated Cheddar cheese
1 tablespoon grated onion	

Canned beans in chile sauce should be available all over the country by now; if by any chance you can't find them, prepare as follows:

¾ cup dried pinto beans, picked over and washed	1 teaspoon oregano
1½ cups water	1 large clove garlic, minced
1½ tablespoons coarse-ground red chile (*chile caribe*)	Salt to taste

Put the beans in the cold water, bring them to a boil, and turn off the heat. Allow them to soak two hours, then bring to a boil again, reduce at once to a simmer, and add the chile, oregano, and garlic, but no salt, which will toughen the beans. Simmer till a bean crushes easily against the side of the pan, from one and a half to three hours, depending on the altitude. Salt to taste. If canned beans are used, heat them to just below boiling. Mash the beans against the side of the pot, a few at a time, until none are left whole. Stir in the grated onion, bring the mixture to just below the boiling point, and slowly thicken with the cheese, stirring slowly and constantly. Best served hot, but very good cold.

For an elaborate Southwestern party, the three dips would be served with cocktails, and the successive courses, including a seafood or avocado cocktail, would be accompanied by beer.

All the normal Eastern cocktails go well with the Southwestern dips; but we are very fond of two tequila drinks, the Margarita and Sangre de los Angeles.

Tequila, by the way, is a variety of a liquor called mescal; in Mexico it is illegal to call mescal tequila unless it comes from the state of Jalisco.

All the mescals are made from the fermented, distilled juice of the maguey or agave plant, called aloe by the British, and often Spanish bayonet in North American.

COCTEL MARGARITA
(*Margarita Cocktail*)
(Serves 1)

2 jiggers (1½ ounce each) tequila (or mescal)	**½ jigger fresh lime juice** **Ice**
1 jigger Cointreau (Controy, Triple Sec, etc.)	**Salt** **½ fresh lime**

Mix the three liquids well with ice. Spread the salt on a plate, rub the edge of a cocktail glass with the half lime and twirl the damp edge of the glass in the salt.
Carefully strain the iced cocktail into the glass, so as not to disturb the salted edge.

The other tequila drink came up from Mexico, from Chapala, explicitly. It was invented by a lady named Sara Nido, who called it Sangre de los Angeles, referring to the denizens of heaven rather than the city in California. Sara has since gone to join *los angeles,* and the name has changed to Sangre de la Viuda, blood of the widow, which Sara indeed was when she concocted her angelic formula.

Sara Nido's hotel, El Nido, was a hospitable place; all the tequila and Sangre you could drink was on the house when you arrived.

You need two glasses, one filled with tequila, and the other with Sangre, which is made in various ways. Frankly, I've forgotten Sara's original recipe, which called for a hot sauce named Bufalo, impossible to obtain in the Estados Unidos, so I make it this way:

SANGRE DE LOS ANGELES
(*Angel's Blood*)

1 quart grapefruit juice	4 tablespoons lemon juice
1 quart tomato juice	Dash soy sauce
2 ounces La Victoria	
salsa verde (Green Hot	
Sauce) *or:*	
1 ten-ounce can mild enchilada sauce	

Mix well. Do not chill. Take a sip of tequila, wash it down with the Sangre.

*   *   *

A *coctel*, in Mexican Spanish, is usually an alcoholic drink; what we call seafood cocktails are *escabeches* or *ceviches*, which can also be spelled *sebiche* or *seviche;* V and B are pronounced alike in the Southwest, and almost alike in Mexico.

Ceviches are made of raw fish or shellfish, reminiscent of Japanese cooking. Time and lime juice will cook seafood without heat.

The people in the northern Southwest got their seafood from the Santa Fe Railroad, which kept icing stations all along the way from Chicago; in the border country, seafood did, and does, come up from the Gulf of California—also called the Sea of Cortez—in delicious profusion.

My favorite Mexican fish is red snapper, called *huachinango* in Mexican, but any good white-fleshed fish will do.

CEVICHE DE PESCADO
(Fresh Fish Cocktail)

1 pound very fresh
white-fleshed fish, boned
and skinned and cut into
1-inch cubes

2 tablespoons lime juice,
preferably from Mexican
small limes *or:*
1 tablespoon Persian
lime juice *and* 1
tablespoon lemon juice

½ cup fairly coarse-
chopped celery

4 tablespoons coarse-ground
red chile (*chile caribe*)

1 teaspoon oregano

Pinch each cumin (*comino*)
and coriander (*cilantro*)

Salt

2 canned tomatoes, drained

Put the fish in a glass or ceramic bowl, and pour on the lime
juice. Turn every ten minutes for three-quarters of an hour. Add

the celery. With a wooden spoon, mix the spices into the tomatoes, crushing the tomatoes as you do so, until you have a smooth purée. Stir the celery and fish into the purée, divide into four cocktail glasses and chill thoroughly before serving.

CEVICHE DE CAMARONES
(*Shrimp Cocktail*)

1 pound shelled and deveined small raw shrimps
3 tablespoons Mexican lime juice *or:*
   2 tablespoons Persian lime juice *and* 1 tablespoon lemon juice
1 medium onion, finely grated
2 canned tomatoes, drained

4 tablespoons coarse-ground red chile (*chile caribe*)
½ clove garlic, pounded or pressed through a garlic press
½ teaspoon oregano
1 pinch coriander (*cilantro*)
1 small pinch thyme (*tomillo*)
1 hard-cooked egg

Marinate the shrimps in the lime or mixed juice until they turn pink, about half an hour.

Stir the onion into the tomatoes, crushing them against the side of the bowl with a wooden spoon; add the chile and continue stirring; then add the other spices, and stir until a smooth sauce is achieved.

Divide into four cocktail glasses and grate the hard-cooked egg on top of each glass for garnish.

Tostados make a good accompaniment for a seafood cocktail. In the Southwest, they can be bought at any grocery store; but if they are not available, it is easy to make your own out of canned or fresh or frozen tortillas (see Chapter 8).

TOSTADOS
(*Crisp Small Tortillas*)

1 cup lard
4 tortillas
Salt

Heat the lard to French-frying heat, approximately 380° F.
Tear the tortillas into pieces about 2 inches square and drop
them into the hot fat a few at a time.
Take them out with a slotted spoon after ten or fifteen seconds,
drain on brown paper, and salt liberally.
Serve cold.

CHAPTER 2

Soup all day long

SOUPS, BOTH DRY AND WET. BROTHS, MEATBALLS

Not many professional horsemen are left in the Southwest, in the opinion of an old-timer. Nowadays, cattle are handled in comparatively small fields cut up by barbed wire, and the cowboys ride to their work in pickup trucks, with the horses haughtily looking over the landscape from the truck body or a trailer.

But twenty, or even fifteen years ago, a lot of the range was still open, and a man could be out three days, or even a week, sleeping on the ground at night, riding a long loop, carrying beans and bacon, flour and coffee and sugar, and shooting a bird or a rabbit to vary the monotonous diet.

The buckaroos who corrupted *vaquero* to title their position—*vaquero* meaning cowman in Spanish—learned a trick from their Mexican and Spanish colleagues that took the kinks out of a body, perhaps no longer young, that had rested on the hard, hard ground and gotten up before dawn to take up a way of life as unyielding as the makeshift bed.

Before going to sleep, feet to the small fire, the trimmings from a rabbit or a few quail or a pheasant—feet, back, wings —were put on the fire with water, maybe a few wild onions, an herb or two.

In the live oak country, we were lucky; a few sticks of green oak put on the fire at night would still be hot eight hours later, and a rider could just put on his roping glove, pick up the pot, and drink. The mesquite or piñon country-men had to build up their fires first, but still, the broth was warm long before coffee could boil.

Lacking fresh meat, the morning broth consisted of mashed-up beans, cubes of bacon, and extra water.

The custom moved into town, where the Mexicans of the southern Southwest give a soup the beautiful name of Soup of Dawn.

CALDO DE ALBOR
(*Dawn Broth*)

4 ounces tomato paste
3 cups strong beef broth
1 slice thoroughly stale
    white bread

¼ pound raw round steak,
    cut into julienne strips
½ teaspoon dry sage

Mix the tomato paste into the barely warm stock, thoroughly. Crumple the bread up fine, and slowly add the mixed broth and tomato paste until the liquid thickens. Bring to a quick boil and then reduce to a slow simmer.

Toss in the beef and sage; stir, simmer till the beef loses its red color, and eat at once.

In northern New Mexico, where the tradition is Spanish rather than Mexican, pork broth is very popular.

CALDO COLADO
(Clear Broth)

2 pounds pork neck bones	1 teaspoon fine-ground red
2 medium onions, chopped	chile
2 tablespoons lard	½ teaspoon dried oregano
1 cup stale tortilla crumbs	1 teaspoon fresh chopped
1 canned whole green chile	mint *or:*
	½ teaspoon dried mint

Cover the neck bones with cold water, between 1½ to 2 quarts. Bring to a boil and then reduce heat at least three times, skimming carefully each time. Then add half the chopped onion and simmer for at least four hours.

Heat the lard in a skillet, add the rest of the onion, and brown slightly. At once add the tortilla crumbs, stir and add the green chile, coarsely minced. Stir in the seasonings, except the mint.

Divide the mixture among four soup bowls, pour on the hot soup, sprinkle with mint, and serve at once.

The dry soup is more of a Mexican dish than it is Spanish, so the closer you are to the border, the more likely you are to run into it. Still, most of the old Spanish families have at least one recipe for a dry soup, probably the following, or a variant of it.

The saffron called for, by the way, is not true saffron, but the New Mexican variety, which is really garnered from safflower plants. These were imported by homesick Spanish priests, and have since escaped and grow wild. I prefer it to Spanish saffron, but the latter will do; perhaps it would be wise to use a little less of the Spanish than you would of the New Mexican.

Green onions grow wild on the mesas of the Southwest, and have a flavor all their own; they most nearly approach a slot between the leek and fresh shallot in flavor, and between garlic and scallions in looks. They give their name to the town of Ajo, Arizona, *ajo* meaning garlic, and to Cebolla, New Mexico, *cebolla* meaning onion.

They can be found only after a warm mesa rain, and in their absence, we use scallions, but leeks would do; use only the white parts, and about 1 leek instead of 4 scallions.

SOPA SECA DE ARROZ
(*Dry Rice Soup*)

2 tablespoons lard or bacon fat	2 cups cooked rice
4 white bulbs of spring or wild onions, finely chopped	2 teaspoons saffron
	½ cup chicken stock, skimmed
	2 hard-cooked eggs

Heat the fat, and gently cook the green onion bulbs; add the rice and stir thoroughly. Moisten the saffron with the chicken stock, add the broth to the rice, divide into four portions, and grate half a hard-cooked egg over each.

The dry soups of the South, in the Mexican tradition, are quite substantial; for a sedentary diet, they might well serve for a main course, especially if they follow a liquid soup, as at border fiestas.

SOPA SECA DE TORTILLAS
(*Dry Tortilla Soup*)

2 tablespoons olive oil	2 cups tomato sauce
2 tablespoons cooking oil, other than olive	½ teaspoon oregano
4 tortillas	4 hard-cooked eggs
1 medium onion, coarsely chopped	¼ pound sliced mild Cheddar cheese

Mix the oils, and fry the tortillas, torn into strips, for about twenty seconds. Remove the tortilla strips with a slotted spoon, and reserve them.

In the same oil, fry the onion until it is transparent; stir in the tomato sauce and oregano and slow boil until the liquid is reduced by half. Slice the eggs fairly thick, and add them and the tortilla strips to the reduced tomato sauce.

Place in an oven preheated to 350° F. and bake one hour. Fifteen minutes before the end of baking, cover with the sliced cheese.

Gazpacho is midway between a dry soup and a wet one, but it is purely Old Spain Spanish. However, a traditional soup from the Sangre de Cristo Mountains in Northern New Mexico may be made into something very like a gazpacho by draining the broth and replacing it with olive oil.

The drained broth makes a wonderful dawn soup.

SOPA DE VERDURAS
(*Vegetable Soup*)

1 cup parched corn *or:*
   1 package frozen
   corn (10–16 ounces)
1 good lamb or mutton
   bone with some lean
   meat left on
2 medium onions, sliced
1 clove garlic, crushed
2 quarts cold water
1 red chile pod, crumbled
2 cups freshly washed
   spinach, packed tight

2 large tomatoes, peeled
   and quartered
4 green squash, thinly
   sliced
1 large pinch ground cloves
   (*clavas*)
1 large pinch dried mint
   (*yerba buena*)
Salt to taste
1 pint olive oil
1 teaspoon lemon juice

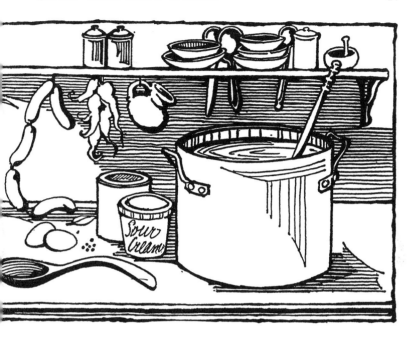

Place the corn, meat bone, onion, and garlic in a heavy kettle; add 2 quarts of cold water, and bring to a boil three times, skimming each time.

Reduce heat to simmer, cover, and cook for two hours (sea level time). Add the other vegetables and the herbs, salt to taste, and cook another fifteen minutes at a simmer.

Drain, and while still hot, stir the oil and lemon juice into the vegetables; chill thoroughly and serve.

The next recipe calls for chorizo, a highly spiced Mexican sausage. Puerto Rican, or Spanish chorizo, sold in the East, is sweeter and different. Many of the chorizos sold in the Southwest come from the Chicago packinghouses, rather amazingly, so butchers in other parts of the United States might be able to get them for you.

There is an Italian pepper sausage that makes a good substitute; or by consulting the Index of this book you will find a recipe for making your own Chorizo al Hogar, a patty of which will do nicely. A chorizo is about the size of a knackwurst.

SOPA DE CHICHAROS
(Unsplit Pea Soup)

1 cup dried round yellow peas, unsoaked	1 whole chorizo
	1½ quarts cold water
1 small yellow onion, sliced	2 cups milk
1 clove garlic, crushed	

Put everything but the milk in 1½ quarts of cold water, and bring it slowly to a boil. Reduce the heat to a simmer and cook at least two hours, till the peas are tender. (If you suspect they have been aged in the store, allow extra time.)

Remove the chorizo, skin it and slice it thin. Reserve the slices.

Put the soup through a colander or ricer, replace the sausage slices, and slowly stir in the milk.

Raise the heat till the milk almost, but not quite, boils, and serve at once.

The garbanzo, sometimes called chick-pea in English, or ceci in Louisiana French, is probably the second-favorite dried legume of Southwesterners. The first, of course, is the small red bean in the south and the pinto bean in the north. Garbanzos are so different from beans that it is safe to serve Chick-pea Soup before a dinner featuring beans.

SOPA DE GARBANZOS
(*Chick-Pea Soup*)

2 cups chick-peas, canned, or soaked overnight if dry	2 tablespoons tomato paste
1½ quarts warm water	1 teaspoon fine-ground red chile
1 small onion, minced	4 rounded tablespoons sour cream
1 clove garlic, crushed and minced	
4 slices bacon, fried, drained, and crumbled	

Put the garbanzos in 1½ quarts warm water, bring to a boil, and reduce to a simmer. Add the onion, garlic, and bacon, and stir once. Slowly add the tomato paste, so as not to reduce the heat. Make a paste of the chile with a little of the water from the pot, and return to the chick-peas.

Cover and let the peas cook until tender but not broken, about 1½ hours at sea level. Serve in preheated individual bowls, with a spoon of sour cream atop each portion.

Tripe is called *menudo* in the Southwest, and has other names in other Spanish-speaking countries—*callos, tripas, cuajar*—a bit of advice that might be useful in dealing with Spanish-speaking butchers.

The honeycomb, called *menudo de casitas*—tripe of little houses—is the best. Nowadays, tripe comes steam-cleaned, and the old-time laborious washing is not necessary.

However, it is advisable to turn the honeycomb face down and cut the fat off the back. This appears as obvious fat and also in long rolls that look like sinews.

Menudo is, in most of the Southwest, traditional for Sunday morning, as it is highly effective as an antidote for hangover. However, non-drinkers don't have to avoid it.

MENUDO NUEVO MEXICANO
(Tripe Soup, New Mexico Style)

1½ pounds lean tripe, cut
into 1-inch squares
1 large onion, thickly sliced
1 green chile, canned or
roasted, chopped

2 quarts water
2 teaspoons dried mint

Put the tripe, onion, and chile into a kettle with 2 quarts of water. Bring to a boil, skim, and simmer for about two hours, or until the tripe cuts with a salad fork.
Divide into four bowls, and sprinkle half a teaspoon of mint on each portion.

MENUDO CON POSOLE
(Tripe Soup with Hominy)

1 pound tripe, cut in
1-inch squares
2 quarts water
1 large white onion, thinly
sliced
2 teaspoons oregano
1 teaspoon fresh-ground
black pepper

Pinch ground cumin
(*comino*) seed
Pinch crumbled coriander
(*cilantro*) leaves
1 ⚹303 can white
hominy

Put the tripe in 2 quarts of water, bring to a boil and skim. Reduce to a simmer, and add the onion, oregano, and other spices.

When you can cut the tripe with a salad fork, add the drained hominy and bring to a quick boil. Serve at once.

Traditionally, the next soup was made with the backbone of a lamb, but modern practice cuts the carcass into quarters, so the lean end of the neck is substituted.

CALDO CON BOLITAS DE LECHE
(Broth with Custard Balls)

THE BROTH:

2 pounds lamb neck, in 1-inch slices	**3 tablespoons chopped parsley**
3 bunches green onions, sliced into 1-inch lengths	**Pinch marjoram**
	2 quarts boiling water

THE CUSTARD BALLS:

2 cups milk	**Additional flour**
½ cup white flour	**1 stick (¼ pound) salted butter**
2 egg yolks	
Pinch thyme (*tomillo*)	

Put the meat, onions, and herbs in the bottom of a heavy kettle; turn heat up high, and pour on 2 quarts of fiercely boiling water. Bring to a boil twice, skimming each time. Reduce heat to a simmer, cover, and cook for at least two hours at sea level.

Remove the bones, scrape off any meat that clings to them, and return the meat to the broth.

While the meat is simmering, prepare the custard balls. Warm the milk in a double boiler until the first bubble appears. At once remove from the heat. Put the flour in a bowl, and gradually add the warm milk, stirring until a smooth paste is achieved.

When all the milk is in the flour, add the slightly beaten egg yolks, and the thyme, and return the double boiler to the stove. Cook slowly, stirring constantly, until the mixture thickens to a point where a toothpick comes out clean. Remove from heat, and cut into balls (about the diameter of a dime) with a melon cutter, two spoons, or your fingers. Roll in the additional flour and refrigerate until the broth is done.

Melt the butter in a frying pan and fry the balls until they are golden brown. Divide the balls among four soup bowls, preheated, and strain the broth over them.

Piñon nuts, *piñones* in Spanish, are the fruit of the characteristic tree of the mesas of the northern tier of the Southwest. They can be bought in any Italian neighborhood; the Italians call them *pignoli*. Though the Italian edible nut pine is a different species from the Southwestern one, the nuts are identical in taste and appearance; use either in the following recipe:

SOPA CON ALBONDIGAS AGRINGADAS
(*Southwestern Meatball Soup*)

1 pound lean round steak	1 pound coarsely ground
4 cups boiling water	hamburger
1 large white onion	Seasoned flour
2 eggs	3 tablespoons shelled
6 saltines	piñon nuts
2 teaspoons oregano	

With a dessert spoon scrape the round steak until it is reduced to a paste. Place in the top of a double boiler and add 4 cups of boiling water. As the meat simmers in the top of the double boiler, peel the onion and grate it coarsely into the soup. Continue cooking, covered, without boiling for at least two hours; more will not hurt.

Meanwhile, make the meatballs by working the eggs, crumbled saltines, and oregano into the coarse-ground hamburger. Roll in the seasoned flour and then press the piñons all over the meatballs, porcupine-style. Refrigerate until half an hour before the soup is done; then drop the meatballs into the broth, one at a time, making sure they do not touch. Cover, and do not uncover until ready to serve; then divide the meatballs among four soup plates, and pour the broth over them.

A more traditional meatball can be boiled and served with any kind of clear soup.

ALBONDIGAS MEXICANAS
(*Mexican Meatballs*)

½ pound raw beef	Pinch cumin (*comino*)
½ pound lean raw pork	Flour
1 egg	Salt
3 teaspoons raw rice	Boiling clear soup (any
1 cup chopped parsley	kind)
(less if dry)	
1 teaspoon fine-ground red	
chile	

Put the meat into a grinder, coarse knife, and grind into a slightly chilled bowl. Add the egg, the rice, the parsley, chile, and cumin and stir thoroughly with a stainless steel fork.

Mix the flour and salt and spread on a plate. Using two tablespoons (fingers will rob the meat of some of its flavor) shape meat into twelve balls and roll them around in the flour till they are completely white.

Drop into boiling soup, cover tightly, and cook at a simmer for half an hour; add five minutes per thousand feet above sea level.

Finally, a tortilla soup. Traditionally, the cheese called for is Monterey Jack, a rather tasteless product when soft enough to grate, and iron-hard by the time it develops flavor. I prefer a Parmesan, or even a Romano.

SOPA DE TORTILLA
(*Wet Tortilla Soup*)

3 tortillas	½ teaspoon dried coriander
4 tablespoons cooking oil	(*cilantro*) leaves
1 onion, chopped	1½ cups grated cheese
2 quarts chicken broth	
4 ounces tomato sauce, canned	

Cut the tortillas into strips an inch wide. Heat the oil to about 350° F. in a heavy skillet, and fry the tortillas a few at a time for fifteen seconds each.

Remove the tortillas with a slotted spoon and put them on brown paper to drain.

Fry the chopped onion in the same oil used for the tortillas, and when the onion is transparent, add the chicken broth and tomato sauce; bring to boiling, reduce the heat, and add the coriander leaves, crumbled.

Simmer, covered, for half an hour, replace the tortillas, and simmer till they are heated through.

Serve with the grated cheese on the side, to be added to individual taste.

CHAPTER 3

Salads, both wild and tame

HERB, CONVENTIONAL, BEAN SALADS,

AND AVOCADO RECIPES

Originally, there were only a few ways of making a living in the Southwest—sheepherding, cattle-tending, trapping, mining or driving on the Chihuahua and, later, Santa Fe trails. There were some farmers, but working the soil was difficult because of Apache and Navajo raids.

All of these lonely pursuits called for a man to travel light, and to be out of touch with any source of supply for weeks and months at a stretch.

Instinct, rather than a knowledge of dietetics, guided the early Southwesterners—Indians, Spanish, Mexicans, and, later, Missouri drovers—to seek out and eat fresh herbs and berries and even roots, not for nourishment, but for the vitamins that they had never heard of.

The Spanish-speaking cattlemen gathered herbs and plants

as they rode, and usually stewed them into greens; when the gringo cowboy came on the scene, he was likely to eat no vegetables at all, until payday, when he rode into a trading post and desperately swallowed a can or two of tomatoes before falling to the drinking that was almost ritual.

But the shepherd, Spanish, Mexican, or Indian, was and still is a great raw herb eater, an eager seeker-out of good-tasting leaves and berries and roots. So the first salad recipe below is from a sheep camp, almost the way an old Basque— called vasco in the Southwest—made it for me.

Almost, but not quite. He used a wild species of *Montia* that I've heard called miner's lettuce, Indian lettuce, and just wild greens in different mountain ranges. Bibb lettuce is the closest thing to it that ever appears in the market.

The sorrel he used was wild, but sorrel is easy to grow in a window box, and delicious in any kind of salad.

ENSALADA DE PASTOR
(*Shepherd's Salad*)

1 medium head Bibb lettuce	1 raw egg
1 bunch watercress	2 tablespoons vinegar
2 cups sorrel leaves, with a few stems	Salt
	Fresh-ground pepper

Tear the lettuce into pieces, trim any coarse leaves out of the watercress, and put all the greens in a colander. Wash them under cold water, tossing with fingers until any possible sand is removed. Swing the greens in a dry towel until dry.

Put in a salad bowl, break the egg over the greens, add the vinegar and toss vigorously. Salt and pepper to taste and serve in individual salad bowls.

Of course, there is a chile salad. Use canned chiles, unless you are a purist, in which case consult the Index to learn how to roast and peel chiles.

ENSALADA DE CHILES VERDES
(Green Chile Salad)

1 clove garlic	4 medium tomatoes
1 medium yellow onion, thinly sliced	1 four-ounce can green chiles, whole
1 tablespoon cider vinegar	Salt to taste

Rub the salad bowl with the peeled garlic, exerting pressure and continuing until the garlic nearly disappears.

Put the onion slices in the bowl and toss them with the vinegar. Allow to stand.

Meanwhile, dip the tomatoes in boiling water for a minute or so, and peel them. Quarter, and put on top of the marinating onion slices.

Remove and discard all the seeds from the chiles. Cut the chiles into long, narrow strips, add to the salad bowl, and toss well, salting to taste.

No oil is needed in this salad, as chiles have a delicate natural oil of their own.

BETABEL FRIOLENTO
(Chilled Beet Salad)

4 large beets, peeled	Salt
1 large bunch celery	Black pepper
1 hard-cooked egg	Paprika
5 tablespoons mayonnaise	1 bunch watercress
1 tablespoon vinegar	

Boil the beets until tender; then scoop out centers with a dessert spoon, leaving a wall about ⅜ inch thick.

Place the beet shells in the coldest part of the refrigerator to chill. Chop the celery and egg and mix thoroughly with the scooped-out beet, adding the mayonnaise and vinegar about halfway through the process. Salt and pepper to taste, and mix again.

Stuff the beet shells with the mixture, and sprinkle the tops with paprika. Return to the refrigerator for at least an hour; longer will not hurt.

Garnish with watercress and serve.

The next recipe sounds as though it had drifted over from California, but it is called a salad of *quelites,* which means greens in New Mexico, rather than *espinaca,* which would be Californian. At any rate, it is fine-tasting.

ENSALADA DE QUELITES
(*Green Salad*)

6 cloves garlic	2 teaspoons red wine
½ cup olive oil	vinegar
2 slices fresh white bread,	Salt
cubed	Black pepper
1 large bunch spinach	

Peel the garlic, and heat the oil in a heavy skillet. Fry the garlic gently, not allowing it to brown, for about five minutes; take the garlic out with a slotted spoon, and discard.

Raise the heat under the oil so that a cube of bread will brown golden in three minutes. Fry all the cubes, remove from the oil, and put on brown paper to drain. Set the oil aside to cool.

Wash the spinach thoroughly, pinch off the leaves, and discard the stalks.

When the oil is thoroughly cool, beat in the vinegar until the mixture is slightly opaque. Salt and pepper to taste, add the spinach leaves, and toss thoroughly. Just before serving, add the croutons, and toss once, only.

So many of the traders and merchants in the Southwest came from Germany, either directly or after one generation in St. Louis or New York, that on the nineteenth century hotel menus potato salad was almost always called kartoffel salad, though I've never seen it called salat, which would be German.

Unfortunately, the recipes are lost. But in Hermosillo, Sonora, the cooking is mixed Mexican and German, and our recipe comes from there; it must closely resemble the kartoffel salads served by Spanish cooks on the old Plaza in Santa Fe and in the hotels of Tucson and Mesilla and Prescott.

ENSALADA DE PAPAS
(*Potato Salad*)

4 tablespoons coarse-ground red chile (*chile caribe*)	1 tablespoon red wine vinegar
1 tablespoon warm water	1 tablespoon brown sugar
2 hard-cooked eggs, sliced	1 pinch dried tarragon
4 medium boiling potatoes	Salt
2 large green apples	Black pepper
¼ cup olive oil	

Work the ground chile into a smooth paste with a tablespoon or so of warm water; the amount needed will depend on how dry the chile is.

Place the egg slices on a flat plate, and spread each slice with the chile paste. Marinate for several hours. Boil the potatoes until tender, peel, and cut into inch cubes. Peel and cube the apples.

Scrape off any chile paste that has not been absorbed by the egg slices. Mix the oil, vinegar, sugar, tarragon, and salt and pepper in a screw-top jar and shake thoroughly. Put the potatoes, eggs, and apples in a salad bowl, pour on the mixed salad dressing, and toss very gently. Chill thoroughly before serving.

Piñon nuts appear again in the next salad dish. Do not wash the cherry peppers; the slight amount of juice in which they were pickled flavors the salad subtly.

ENSALADA DE EJOTES
(Green Bean Salad)

1 ✕300 or ✕303 can French-cut string beans	¼ cup cooking oil
	2 tablespoons white vinegar
1 large red onion, sliced very thin	2 tablespoons shelled piñon nuts
1 hot or 2 sweet pickled cherry peppers	Salt

Drain the beans carefully and put them in a bowl.
Add the sliced onions.
Chop the pickled peppers, catching the juice, and add to the onion-bean mixture. Toss twice.
Add all the other ingredients, salting to your own taste, toss and place all in a mason jar. Chill at least a full day, turning the jar upside down every time you open the refrigerator.

In the fall, in the Southwest, the bell peppers turn red, and are perfectly beautiful. Actually, they taste very little different from green bell peppers, just slightly milder; but if the following recipe is made with one red and one green pepper, its aesthetic value is increased.

ENSALADA DE PIMIENTOS DULCES
(Sweet Pepper Salad)

2 large bell peppers, preferably one green and one red	1 corn tortilla, torn into small pieces
Salt	1 teaspoon fine-ground red chile
1 medium yellow onion	½ cup cider vinegar
4 slices fat bacon	4 small green tomatoes

Top the peppers, remove all seeds and white veins, and cut the pepper meat crosswise into fairly thick slices. Put in a bowl with a little salt. Slice the onion.

Chop the bacon into ¼-inch squares and try it out slowly in a heavy skillet.

As the fat appears, add the sliced onion and sauté until it is transparent. Add the tortilla pieces. If any of the tortilla or bacon bits begin to turn black, take them out with a slotted spoon and add them to the pepper bowl.

When the bacon has tried out, remove it and any remaining tortilla or onion, and add to the bell peppers.

When the fat is clear, reduce the heat under the skillet as low as possible, and start stirring the red chile into the fat.

When a smooth paste is achieved, dilute it with the vinegar, all at once. The vinegar will boil up immediately. Scrape the contents of the skillet into the bowl, and toss vigorously. Add the green tomatoes, quartered, toss once more, and serve either at once, or chilled.

Cauliflower, eaten raw, is an Anglo dish. Spanish and Mexican people boil theirs thoroughly before breaking the head up into flowerets. Suit yourself; flavor your cauliflower raw, blanched, or cooked in the following manner:

COLIFLOR FRIA
(*Cold Cauliflower*)

3 tablespoons shelled piñon
nuts
1 teaspoon whole black
peppercorns
1 clove garlic, peeled
1 teaspoon coarse-ground
red chile (*chile caribe*)

½ cup olive oil
¼ cup vinegar
3 cups cauliflower flowerets,
cooked or raw

Pound the piñons, peppercorns, and garlic clove in a mortar, moving always in the same direction. When a paste is established, add the chile and go around a time or two more.

Still stirring in the same direction, begin dripping in the oil very slowly, as in making mayonnaise.

When all the oil is in, add the vinegar; not as much care is needed in stirring during this step.

Put the cauliflower in a bowl and add the sauce; toss with care so as not to break up the flowerets, until each bit is thoroughly covered with the sauce.

Late additions to the Southwestern diet are grapefruit and avocados. Arizona turns out grapefruit as delicious as can be found, and avocados come in from California; Mexico grows even better ones.

The *salsa verde* (green sauce) used in this recipe can be bought bottled or canned; you can make your own from the recipe in the chapter on sauces; see the Index.

AGUACATE Y PAMPLEMUSA
(*Avocado and Grapefruit*)

2 ripe, medium avocados	1 tablespoon lemon juice
1 grapefruit, preferably pink	1 teaspoon *salsa verde*
½ cup ketchup	(Green Hot Sauce)

Cut the avocados in half and peel; discard the pits. Peel the grapefruit and separate into its natural divisions. Put each half avocado on a salad plate and surround it with the grapefruit sections. Mix the ketchup, lemon juice, and green sauce thoroughly and pour over the grapefruit and in the hollow of the avocado halves.

ENSALADA DE PRIMAVERA
(*Spring Salad*)

4 avocados	1 teaspoon cooking oil, not
12 scallions	olive
2 cooked beets, peeled	4 tortillas
½ cup cider vinegar	
1 tablespoon coarse-ground red chile (*chile caribe*)	

Quarter the avocados and peel them. Put four quarters in the bottoms of four salad bowls, and place in the freezing compartment of the refrigerator for about fifteen minutes.

Meanwhile, chop the scallions, using the same amount of green stalk as you have white bulb.

Slice the beets and quarter the slices. Mix with the onions, and divide among the chilling avocado bowls.
Warm the vinegar, to just above room temperature, not more than 100° F.
Slowly stir the warmed vinegar into the chile, until they form a smooth paste. Pour into the chilled bowls, add ¼ teaspoon oil to each bowl. Mix lightly, rechill for a few minutes, and serve with the tortillas on the side.

Too many people in the Eastern United States don't know about the chick-pea, a simple masterpiece of nature. Louisiana French people, as mentioned before, call them cecis, and in the Southwest we name them garbanzos. The canned are every bit as good as the dried that you soak overnight and simmer to tenderness.

GARBANZOS ENCURTIDOS
(*Soused Chick-peas*)

2 cups cooked chick-peas, or 1 ✕300 can	1 cup French dressing
1 very large white onion, thinly sliced	½ teaspoon freshly ground black pepper

Heat the chick-peas till they steam; stir, remove from the stove, drain and stir in the onion slices, letting them break if they want to.
Before the mixture cools to room temperature, stir in the French dressing and fresh pepper. Chill for half an hour and serve. This may also be served as an appetizer.

CHAPTER 4

A few piquant sauces

CHILE SAUCES, BOTH TABLE AND KITCHEN TYPES

In Spanish, *picante* means spicy hot, and *caliente* hot from a flame; this for the advice of phrase-book travelers.

To this may be added advice on what to do if you take a bite of food that is too *picante:* don't slosh ice water around in your mouth. It will do no good. Banana is best, anything sweet second best, and plain bread or tortilla next in efficacy.

Northern New Mexicans delight in scorching their palates with chile and then cooling them with preserves. Jams and jellies, however, are seldom served with the meal in the southern Southwest. But, then, the food there is usually rather bland, with the flavor furnished in a side dish of sauce.

Some of the following sauces are always served as side dishes, some always as condiments in cooking, some can be used either way. In later chapters they will be called for as needed, and the reader can get back to the recipe through the Index.

Any of these sauces will freeze, and all will keep for a
week or more in the refrigerator, so they can be prepared
well in advance. Each recipe should make enough sauce to
serve four people generously. The first one is always served as a side dish, except in
seafood and avocado cocktails.

SALSA PICANTE
(*Hot Sauce*)

SAUCE NUMBER ONE—*Salsa Número Uno*

2 medium canned tomatoes, drained	1 cup vinegar
4 tablespoons coarse-ground red chile (*chile caribe*)	Salt
1 medium onion, coarsely grated	Pinch each oregano and cumin (*comino*)

Mash the tomatoes with a fork and stir in the chile thoroughly.
Marinate the onion in the vinegar.
Let both stand for half an hour; mix in the salt and spices and
stir well. Refrigerate and serve as a side dish.

SALSA DE CHILE CARIBE
(*Coarse-ground Red Chile Sauce*)

SAUCE NUMBER TWO—*Salsa Número Dos*

2 tablespoons oil or lard	¼ teaspoon oregano
1 small onion, chopped	6 tablespoons coarse-ground red chile (*chile caribe*)
1 clove garlic, minced	Pinch each cumin (*comino*) and coriander (*cilantro*)
1 tablespoon white wheat flour	
½ cup cold water	

Heat lard or oil moderately hot and fry the onion and garlic until transparent, but not brown.

Sprinkle the flour over the fried onion and stir; slowly add the water, continuing to stir till a smooth paste is achieved; then stir in the seasoning slowly, while continuing to cook the sauce. Serve warm as a side dish, or use in cooking as needed.

The next sauce is from the south, and uses two kinds of chiles. The directions for preparing them are tedious; the process of skinning dried chiles can be avoided by using a blender. After the chiles are soaked, they are whirred with a cup or so of warm water, breaking up the skins into harmless bits.

If you follow the traditional method, outlined below, wear long rubber gloves; the chile can get into your bloodstream through the thin skin on your wrists and make you uncomfortably warm.

A long soak in a cold tub will counteract this condition, but the cure is not very pleasant, either.

If you have lived in Mexico or in a small border town, the aroma of this sauce cooking will fill you with nostalgia; it is the most Mexican of sauces.

SALSA DE DOS CHILES
(*Two Chile Sauce*)

SAUCE NUMBER THREE—*Salsa Número Tres*

3 chiles *pasillas*
3 chiles *anchos*
1 small onion
2 cloves garlic
3 stalks fresh *or* ½ teaspoon dried coriander (*cilantro*)

2 tablespoons olive oil or lard
Pinch each oregano and cumin (*comino*)

Put the dried chiles in 2 quarts of tepid water and allow to soak for half an hour. Then rub them gently between your fingers until the skin slips off them. Discard the skins and press the chiles and their water through a coarse sieve.

Chop the onion, garlic, and coriander together and fry them in the olive oil or lard till the onion is transparent.

Add the chile water and pulp and the other seasonings, and cook down to 3 cups, gently, stirring as needed.

Serve warm, or use in cooking.

SALSA COLORADA OSCURA
(*Dark Red Sauce*)

SAUCE NUMBER FOUR—*Salsa Número Quatro*

1 clove whole garlic	3 tablespoons fine-ground
2 tablespoons cooking oil	red chile
or lard	Large pinch oregano
1 medium onion, minced	Small pinch coriander
fairly fine	(*cilantro*)
1 pound fresh (or canned)	
peeled tomatoes	

Fry the whole garlic in the oil until garlic begins to turn dark; remove and discard. Add the onion to the hot fat and cook until it is transparent.

Push the tomatoes through a sieve into the cooking onions, stir thoroughly and continue to stir as the chile and herbs are blended in.

Reduce the heat to a simmer and cook the sauce until it is reduced by a third.

Serve chilled or warm, or use in cooking.

The next sauce is the favorite one of Rosalea, who runs the famous Pink Adobe in Santa Fe. The combination of green and red chiles makes it unique in taste and appearance.

SALSA DE SANTA FE
(Sante Fe Chile Sauce)

SAUCE NUMBER FIVE—*Salsa Número Cinco*

1 large white onion	1 ten-ounce can solid-pack
2 tablespoons cooking oil	tomatoes
1 four-ounce can green	Large pinch oregano
chiles	Small pinch cumin (*comino*)
1 tablespoon fine-ground	
red chile	

Slice the onion thickly and sauté in the oil till transparent. Remove as many seeds from the chiles as seems advisable, remembering that they carry most of the heat, and chop the chiles very coarsely. Add them to the sautéeing onion. Stirring steadily, add the other ingredients, and reduce the heat to a very gentle boil, one that can be stopped by stirring. Cook for half an hour. Serve chilled or warm, or use in cooking.

Next, two straight green chile recipes, for use as table condiments. The really elegant table should have a dish of green and a dish of red *salsa picante* furnished.

SALSA PICANTE VERDE
(Green Hot Sauce)

SAUCE NUMBER SIX—*Salsa Número Seis*

2 cups white vinegar, wine
or cider type
1 large white onion, thinly
sliced
4 small, green tomatoes,
very firm
1 four-ounce can green
chiles

1 teaspoon fresh chopped
parsley or ½ teaspoon
dried
1 teaspoon dried ground
turmeric
Pinch each oregano and
cumin (*comino*)
Salt

Warm the vinegar to the boiling point, remove from the heat
and place the sliced onion in it. Allow to cool for an hour.
Slice the tomatoes, unpeeled, very thin; quarter the slices and
add to the marinated onion. Let stand for another half hour.
Remove as many seeds as desired from the chiles—remembering
that they carry most of the heat—which should then be chopped
rather thoroughly. Add the chile and herbs and spices to the
onion-tomato mixture and whip thoroughly with a whisk or eggbeater; a slow blender can be used.
Salt to taste, and chill; keep cold till used, as chile loses its flavor
at room temperature.

SALSA DE CHILES FRESCAS
(Fresh Chile Sauce)

SAUCE NUMBER SEVEN—*Salsa Número Siete*

4 fresh green chiles
1 tablespoon salt
1 large onion, coarsely
chopped

2 cloves garlic, peeled

Put the chiles in a very hot oven, about 450° F., until they blister. Or, lay them over the flame of a gas stove, turning constantly, until blisters appear all over them. At once wrap in a wet towel and allow them to stand for twenty minutes.

Meanwhile, mix the salt and the onion and let it stand, too.

Unwrap the chiles; the papery outer skin should now peel off easily. Split the chiles, and remove as many seeds as seems necessary, since the seeds carry most of the heat. Chop the chiles, discarding the stems.

Put the onion in a colander to drain.

Roast the peeled garlic cloves, whole, in a heavy, hot skillet for five minutes, tossing occasionally to prevent burning.

Chop the garlic and mix with the drained onion and chopped chiles.

Serve chilled, and keep in the refrigerator between servings.

The next recipe calls for a secret ingredient, zucchini, which completely disappears, but lends a smoothness and elegance to the sauce. Small flower squash, white or yellow, can be used, but with some loss in appearance.

SALSA VERDE DE PLAZA
(*Country Green Sauce*)

SAUCE NUMBER EIGHT—*Salsa Número Ocho*

4 small zucchinis, preferably with flowers

2 medium white onions, sliced

1½ tablespoons cooking oil

4 stalks fresh coriander (*cilantro*) or 1 tablespoon dried

2 large stalks watercress

1 cup boiling water

1 four-ounce can green chiles

Slice the zucchinis very thin, flowers and all; do the same with the white onions. Sauté in just enough oil to cover until the onions turn clear; then chop and add the fresh coriander, if you can get it, and the watercress, chopped, being sure that the latter has no coarse threads in it; it shouldn't if it is fresh. Add the cup of boiling water, and simmer for at least twenty minutes. Then add the chiles, chopped coarsely, and with some of the seeds removed to reduce the piquancy; but you will find that the squash absorbs some of the pepperiness.

Simmer another ten minutes, stirring from time to time.

There are other sauces used in the Southwest, but they are specialized, used in one or two dishes only, and will be described when we get to those dishes. *Mole* and *pipian* fall into that category; I've never seen them used on anything but poultry. When you see *frijoles en mole* on a menu, the beans will just be in a good red chile sauce, such as Sauce Number Two, rather than in the elaborate *salsa mole* that goes on turkey.

CHAPTER 5

To refry or not?

BEANS, THE HEART OF SOUTHWESTERN COOKING

Mexicans and Southwesterners are not the only people in the world who feel that life could not be endured without dried legumes. Middle Europe has the split pea and the lentil; Italy the white and kidney bean; New Orleans eats red beans with rice; the Chinese sprout their soy beans or make sauce out of them, while the Japanese make them into bean curd; the English sing about pease porridge, hot or cold, and what would France be without cassoulet?

But in the Southwest, the bean plays a much bigger part in daily life than it does anyplace else I've ever heard of, except Mexico.

It has already been mentioned that there are two broad life zones in the Southwest, Upper Sonoran, the piñon and juniper country; and Lower Sonoran, the mesquite country or its counterpart in New Mexico, the bear grass land.

There are other life zones, in fact all of them except tropical, but few people live in the higher ones, the ponderosa pine, Douglas fir, and so on up to Alpine. When the last piñon disappears and the bear grass sotol dots the country, the botanist knows he's passed from northern to southern New Mexico. The linguistic ethnologist listens for the transition; when more Aztec than English is in the Spanish, he's in Lower Sonoran country. The turkey is *el turqué* in the north, *el guajalote* in the south, and *el pavo* in Spain.

I submit that the easiest way to determine where you are is to eat in the home of someone with a Spanish name. If your host apologizes because the beans are refried, *frijoles refritos,* you are still in the north; if he apologizes because the beans are not refried, you are in the south.

In the upper country only leftover beans are refried; in the mesquite land only lazy cooks—incredibly lazy cooks—serve plain boiled *frijoles.*

If the beans are called free-hole Mexican beans, you are among Texans, but even they do not take their legumes lightly. Beans and biscuits, flapjacks and country-fried steak were the only dishes expected from the old-time bunkhouse cook. Many of their diners lived to be thirty or even more, thirty-one or -two.

Traditionally, it was the Southwestern sun that made the riders' skins so leathery. Not so; it was cowboy coffee, working from the inside out, and held in place by thick layers of beans.

FRIJOLES ESTILO PALOMAR
(*Palomar-style Beans*)

½ pound King City pink beans	½ cup beef jerky
1½ quarts water	2 pounds beef shin
1 cup chopped yellow onion	2 tablespoons *chilepequins* (bird peppers), dried or pickled

Soak the beans overnight, or, in an emergency, put them in 1½ quarts of water, bring to a boil, let them cool and stand two hours.

Then put everything else in, and simmer, making sure that the water doesn't boil away, until a bean can be crushed with a spoon. This should take three to six hours, depending on how long the beans have been drying, and on your altitude.

All the dried legumes, except lentils and peas, take longer to cook when they are old; for this reason it is wise to cook them the day before you want to eat them. Of course, when you're cooking for a crew, the process is continuous; one mess of beans is soaking while a second is cooking and a third being eaten.

All beans—it is not so true of peas and lentils—suffer from high heat, except for the original boiling that takes the place of overnight soaking. Let them take their time, at an even simmer.

The *chilepequins* are tiny, very hot peppers, sometimes called bird peppers, *pajaritos*, or *chiletepins*. East or West, they are easy to find pickled, in shaker bottles; the idea is to shake the vinegar they were pickled in onto your food. But for beans, they can be fished out, if the shaker top is removable, usually the case these days.

The bolita has just about disappeared from the New Mexico scene in the last few years. It is a small brown bean, perfectly round, and it used to be a favorite crop in the little cold valleys north of Santa Fe. Its peculiar virtues are that it has a short growing season, essential in those valleys, and it cooks at a low heat and a high altitude.

But as a cash crop it was a poor one, and when subsistence farming is supplemented with work in Los Alamos or Santa Fe or on the federal highway program, the pinto bean is so inexpensive to buy that bolita farming is just too much trouble.

The little brown mainstay had a different flavor, and will undoubtedly come back as a fiesta dish, a luxury, just as those Indians who formerly subsisted largely on acorn meal now only go through the laborious job of leaching, grinding, and blanching the oak nuts for a saint's day party, or a wedding.

Here's the best way I know to cook bolitas. It can be used for any other kind of dried bean: pintos, pinks, reds, kidneys, navies. I even used Dutch black ones once.

As in all dried bean recipes, the beans have to be soaked overnight, or softened with the shortcut quick boil, two-hour soak method described in Palomar-style Beans.

Easterners will prefer using fresh or homogenized milk; after you've been in the West awhile, the taste of canned cow milk becomes pleasant. Elderly and wealthy ranchers cause scenes in French-type New York restaurants by demanding it in their coffee instead of cream.

BOLITAS CON LECHE
(*Beans with Milk*)

¾ cup dried beans, soaked
  overnight
2 quarts cold water
Salt
2 teaspoons flour
3 tablespoons bacon
  drippings
½ cup chopped yellow
  onion

¾ cup cubed raw potatoes
1 four-ounce can green
  chiles
1 ten-ounce can solid-pack
  tomatoes
1½ cups milk, fresh or
  canned diluted with 1½
  cups water

Start the beans in 2 quarts of cold water; when they begin to
simmer, add salt.

When the beans are almost done, mix the flour with the bacon drippings, and thicken the bean broth with this roux. Then add everything else—the chiles should be chopped coarsely—and cook till the potatoes are done.

It may come as a shock, but Mexicans and Mexican-Americans seldom cook chile, either red or green, with their beans. There is always a dish of *salsa picante* (Sauce Number One, Six, or Seven in the Index) on the table; or one of the other dishes will have a sauce that can be slipped over on the *frijoles*.

Or, perhaps, there will be a dish of pickled *jalapeños* available, one of which can be cut up and mixed with the backbone of the meal. These are shaped like large acorns, and are hot as Death Valley in August; their seeds taste as though they could cut through an express company safe.

Often, however, beans on a Mexican menu come—usually refried—as a penultimate dish, just before the dessert, and are eaten unpeppered to clear the palate after a spicy main dish.

FRIJOLES MEXICANOS
(*The Backbone of Mexico*)

| 3 cups water | ½ cup bacon drippings |
| 1 cup small red beans | Salt |

Heat 3 cups of unsalted water, lukewarm; just before it simmers, put in the beans.

Simmer till a bean can be burst against the side of the pot. Then heat the bacon fat until it spits when a drop of water is flicked in.

Now take a slotted spoon and transfer beans to the fat, mashing them well against the skillet bottom; continue till the beans and fat have made a roux that is dry and solid.

Dissolve this with juice from the bean pot till it is completely smooth and lumpless, and then stir this broth back into the bean pot. Now add salt to taste, and cook all another few minutes.

The people of the Lower Sonoran would be shocked at the Upper Sonoran habit of thickening beans with flour. Beans and bean cookery are passionate things; I would not give 5 pounds of King City (California) beans for all the pintos in the world, and people who come out here from New Orleans have their relatives back home mail them little red beans, sometimes air mail special delivery.

But to me they taste just like Mexican reds; a shade of taste difference is lost to me, which is a pity.

In New Orleans beans are usually served with white rice.

NEW ORLEANS RED BEANS
(*Frijoles Criollos*)

1 cup red beans	**1 bay leaf**
1½ cups cold water	**¼ cup butter**
½ cup chopped red onion	**Salt**
1 carrot, grated	**Black pepper**

Simmer the beans with the onion, carrot, and bay leaf till tender. Remove the bay leaf, drain the beans, and stir in the butter; season with salt and pepper to taste.

Here is another New Mexican way of cooking beans, almost always pintos:

FRIJOLES MONTES
(*Mountain Beans*)

1 clove garlic	½ cup diced salt pork
1½ quarts cold water	Large pinch oregano
1 teaspoon brown sugar	(optional)
1 cup pinto beans	Salt

Mince the garlic and put it and the sugar into cold water; heat. As the water begins to simmer, slowly add the beans. About an hour before they are done, add the salt pork, the oregano, if used, and a little salt. When completely done, add more salt to taste.

Any of the previous recipes will do for refrying. This is how:

FRIJOLES REFRITOS
(*Mexican Delight*)

3 cups cooked and mashed beans
Cooking oil, lard, or beef fat

Remash the mashed beans into the hot fat, turning constantly until crisp.

I've never heard *refritos* called fried in either language; they are always *refritos* or refried, though the frying has been done only once.

If it is done more than twice, they are called *chinitos,* little Chinese, for some reason that eludes research. The more times beans are fried, the crisper they become.

Refritos con queso are made by melting Monterey Jack cheese, cubed, into the beans as they finish frying. This is pure Mexican; I prefer using a sharp Cheddar or even grated Romano cheese.

Fancier bean dishes involve meat. Here is a New Mexican way of making a main dish:

FRIJOLES SABROSOS
(*Savory Beans*)

3 pounds pork neck bones	1 quart plain cooked beans
3 tablespoons lard	(pintos, reds, or pinks)
1 medium yellow onion,	½ cup grated Cheddar
chopped	cheese
1 cup Sauce Number Two	4 tablespoons fresh bread
2 eggs	crumbs

Boil the neck bones, starting in cold water, till the meat falls off. Strain the meat out, allow it to dry, and fry it in the lard with the onion. Skim the broth and boil it down to 1 cup. Add the chile sauce.

Whip the eggs lightly, and stir into the cold beans; add the cheese and bread crumbs, then stir vigorously together with the meat and onion mixture.

Butter or grease a baking pan and put the mixture in it without packing down. Pour the broth-sauce over all and bake at 350° F. for an hour.

Beans can be fine for a Sunday breakfast, or a weekday breakfast on a camping trip; the following dish is a little heavy for the start of a sedentary day:

FRIJOLES DE ALBOR
(*Beans of Dawn*)

1 large onion, minced	1 quart unfried beans,
Cooking fat or oil	cooked
4 teaspoons fine-ground	8 eggs
chile	8 tortillas

Fry the onion until transparent in the fat or oil; add the ground chile and then the beans.

When the mixture is bubbling hot, lower to just below boiling and poach the eggs in it.

Serve in bowls, each lined with a tortilla, 2 eggs, and a fourth of the bean mixture to a diner. Serve extra tortillas on the side.

The big lima-type beans, sometimes called horse beans in the United States, are called *favas* along the border, and *habas* in the north of the Southwest. Around Tesuque, New Mexico, I've heard them called Aztec beans, a very good name for them.

They are good with country ham, especially the Spanish-type country ham, harder and drier than Smithfield or Kentucky or Missouri ham. If you use a soft, packinghouse ham in the following recipe, I'd advise cutting it thin and frying it out in a slow, dry skillet, as commercial hams are usually hung in a damp room for some time to increase their moisture content. Frying takes the water out and crisps the ham to a satisfactory state.

FAVAS BORRACHAS
(Drunken Horse Beans)

1 strip bacon	1 cup water
1 medium red onion,	1 cup cubed ham
chopped	2 tablespoons chopped fresh
1 clove garlic, minced	or 1 teaspoon dried
2 cups pre-soaked fava	oregano
beans	1 teaspoon dried coriander
1 twelve-ounce bottle	(*cilantro*)
Mexican light beer	

In a skillet that can be covered, fry out the bacon; remove it and crumble.

Fry the onion and garlic lightly in the bacon fat.

Add the beans and half the beer, with a cup of water; put in the other ingredients, cover tightly, and simmer.

When the beans are done, pour in the other half bottle of beer, and mash enough beans against the side of the pan to thicken the liquid.

The chick-pea, or garbanzo, is a lovely, lovely thing. It can often be bought canned, in which case, of course, the instructions to pre-soak should be disregarded, and the anticipated cooking time cut down. A recipe has already been given in the salad chapter for marinating garbanzos in French dressing in Garbanzos Encurtidos. They may also be served as an appetizer.

The *chorizos* are Mexican sausages; a substitute is given if you can't buy them.

GARBANZOS EN CHILE VERDE
(*Chick-peas in Green Chile Sauce*)

4 *chorizos or:*	½ pound pre-soaked
4 country pork	garbanzos *or:*
sausages and 2 teaspoons	2 ten-ounce cans
Texas chili powder	pre-cooked garbanzos
2 cups Sauce Number Five	Salt

Skin and fry the sausages in their own fat; crumble the meat with
a fork, add the chili powder if gringo sausages are used.
Pour in the Sauce Number Five and add the garbanzos. If necessary add water, but gabanzos do not take as much as most dried
legumes.
Simmer till done; salt and serve.

Garbanzos, canned or cooked in plain water, are fine with a
4-ounce can of chopped green chiles mixed in.
Or sprinkled with crumbled-up jerky, or tried-out bacon.

GARBANZOS AL HORNO
(*Baked Garbanzos*)

4 cups cooked garbanzos	4 eggs
1 teaspoon oregano	½ pound (1 cup) butter or
1 pinch dried coriander	margarine
(*cilantro*)	
1 teaspoon fine-ground	
red chile	

Mix the flavorings into the garbanzos and put them through a
potato ricer or a coarse sieve.

Separate the eggs, and stir the yolks into the garbanzos. Whip the whites stiff and dry, then fold them in carefully. Butter a baking dish, put in the mixture, and spread the rest of the butter on top in lumps.

Bake at 350° F. for half an hour.

The old Southwest, of course, had little refrigeration. Santa Fe and Phoenix, Prescott, Albuquerque, and perhaps Tucson had ice plants, often in connection with breweries. But most ranches, mountain villages, crossroads general stores, and trading posts had to eat warm-weather meat at once or see it spoil.

Especially lamb and veal.

Like Mexicans, Spaniards, and Italians, the mountain Spanish liked their meat as young as possible. And since sheep and goats have their young in the spring, when weather can suddenly turn warm, traditional uses were found for every part of the small carcass.

Most of the resulting dishes will come in the meat section, but the shanks of a kid or a suckling lamb are so small that the chick-peas with which they were cooked were the main dish; the meat was just flavoring. One good lamb shank, of ordinary market size, will take the place of the two called for below.

GARBANZOS DE PASTOR
(*Shepherd's Chick-peas*)

4 green onions	½ pound chick-peas,
1 small lump lamb's fat,	pre-soaked
preferably from kidney	Salt
2 suckling or 1 market	1 teaspoon saffron, heaping
lamb shank	if of the New Mexico
	variety

Chop the onions fine and put them and the fat in a heavy pot. Slowly try the fat, and brown the shank or shanks, on all sides.

Add the chick-peas and enough water to cover them.

Simmer, adding more water if necessary, till tender.

Salt to taste. Dissolve the saffron in a little warm water and stir in.

CHAPTER 6

The almost mystical egg

AS COOKED BY MEXICANS, SPANISH, AND OTHER
SOUTHWESTERNERS

Eggs mean so much to Spanish-speaking people that they
often receive highly poetic names: starred eggs, *huevos es-
trellados,* for fried eggs; spiritual egg, *huevo espiritual,* for
an eggnog.

The best-known Mexican or Southwestern egg dish is the
breakfast plate of *huevos rancheros,* rancher's eggs. They are
cooked differently in the north than in the south, and the
gachupins, Spaniards who are likely to run delicatessen stores
in Mexican-American neighborhoods, like a dish made with
pimentos and olive oil, worth trying.

Unlike other recipes in this book, the directions in this
chapter are for an individual serving, unless otherwise speci-
fied.

HUEVOS RANCHEROS NORTENSES
(*Eggs Northern Ranch Style*)

1 tortilla	1 four-ounce can green
2 eggs	chiles, with seeds removed
2 tablespoons lard	to control the heat, if
Salt	desired
1 medium onion, chopped	1 large pinch sage
1 tomato from a solid-pack	Pinch coriander (*cilantro*)
can	

Lay the tortilla on a breakfast plate and place it in a warming oven at 200° F.

Fry the eggs in the hot lard, salt them to taste, and carefully remove them with a slotted pancake turner; place them on the tortilla and replace the plate in the oven. Fry the chopped onion until it is clear, and add the tomato; mash it with a wooden spoon and add the chile and seasonings.

Stir until mixture thickens a little, pour over the eggs and serve.

HUEVOS RANCHEROS DE LA FRONTERA
(*Ranch Eggs, Border Style*)

3 tablespoons cooking oil	2 tablespoons coarse-
1 tortilla	ground red chile
2 eggs	(*caribe*)
1 clove garlic, crushed	1 six-ounce can tomato
and minced	sauce
2 dried *chilepequins*	1 tablespoon tomato paste
(bird peppers) *or:*	1 teaspoon oregano

Heat the oil in the bottom of a skillet; spread the tortilla in the hot oil and leave it there till it blisters.

Lift the tortilla with a slotted pancake turner and let the oil drain

back into the skillet. Slide the tortilla onto a plate and keep at
200° F. in the oven.

Fry the eggs on one side, and carefully place them on the
tortilla. Preferably, they should be underdone, as they will continue to cook in the warming oven while the sauce is made.

Put the finely-minced garlic and the crushed or chopped little
chiles (or the *chile caribe*) in the hot oil, and as soon as the
garlic starts to brown, add the tomato sauce. Stir as the sauce
heats up and then slowly add the tomato paste and the oregano.
Simmer all for about ten minutes, pour over the eggs and serve.

HUEVOS RANCHEROS ESTILO GACHUPIN
(*Ranch Eggs, Spain Style*)

3 cloves garlic, crushed and minced	1 two-ounce jar pimentos
4 teaspoons olive oil	Pinch saffron
2 ripe tomatoes	2 eggs

Brown the garlic in the oil, add the tomatoes and crush them
with a wooden spoon; chop the pimentos coarsely, and add them.
Spoon out a little of the sauce, add the saffron to it, and return
to the sauce when the saffron softens.

Break each egg into a cup and slip it into the simmering sauce.
Poach the eggs until done to taste and serve.

The desire to have something sweet with a sharp sauce, so strong among Spanish-speaking people elsewhere, such as in Cuba, is obviously behind a sauce for fried eggs:

HUEVOS DULCES Y PICANTES
(*Sweet and Hot Eggs*)

1 ripe tomato, chopped	2 tablespoons brown sugar
1 red onion, chopped	Juice 1 large orange
1 green chile, chopped	2 eggs
1 teaspoon fine-ground red chile	1 tablespoon oil for frying eggs

Mix all the ingredients except the eggs, chopping everything very fine. Do not cook.
Fry the eggs, or scramble them, and pour the juice over.

Egg fritters are much eaten by the old-timers. The name means a clumsily built small tower. The recipe is for four, and can be used for poaching fritters in any of the hot chile sauces listed in the Index; but if this is done, they should not be drained; instead they should be left in the pot at a simmer until it is time to eat them.

TORREJAS
(*Egg Fritters*)

6 eggs	2 tablespoons whole wheat flour
Cooking oil or fat	
Salt	2 tablespoons breakfast bran

Separate eggs and beat the whites as stiff as possible without drying them out. Beat and salt the yolks and fold in the whites and the flour and bran.
Heat the fat or oil medium hot, not smoking.
Drop the batter by tablespoons into the hot fat, for about four minutes. Remove with a slotted spoon and drain on brown paper.

Mexican French bread is absolutely wonderful; the bakers use flour that has not been over-chemicalized. If there is a Mexican bakery anywhere, try it, but do not buy more than a day's supply at a time, as the untreated flour does not supply any artificial resistance against staleness.

The following recipe can, of course, be made with *norteamericano* rolls. This recipe is also for four people.

HUEVOS AL NIDO
(*Eggs in the Nest*)

4 eggs	Pinch oregano
4 French rolls	Pinch parsley
2 tablespoons butter	Olive oil, preferably
4 tablespoons cream	California
1 teaspoon fine-ground	
red chile	

Separate the eggs, carefully. Slice off the top of each roll, and remove the soft inside, being careful not to tear the walls. Butter the inside of the rolls to make them waterproof.
Put a tablespoon of cream in each roll, and then slip a yolk in on top of it. Beat the whites a little and divide them among the rolls.
Mix the chile and herbs and divide them among the 4 rolls, on top of the egg whites.
Heat the olive oil, in a small skillet, to just below the smoking

point. Put the cut-off tops back on the rolls and lay them in the hot oil.

Now take a large spoon and start basting; do not stop until the eggs are done, about five minutes.

If the olive taste is too strong, drain the nests before serving, but they are just to my taste served very hot and oily.

The bunkhouse cook at a ranch I used to visit would fill an omelet with fried, cubed potatoes and call it a Spanish omelet. He insisted his grandfather was from Spain, and had told him that that was the only true omelet of Spain.

Could be, but the following recipe is much more common in the Southwest. The sauce can be used over scrambled eggs as well. Recipe is for four.

SALSA POR HUEVOS EN TORTA
(*Spanish Omelet Sauce*)

6 medium tomatoes
2 tablespoons olive oil or
  lard
2 medium onions,
  coarsely chopped
1 four-ounce can green
  chiles, seeded to reduce
  heat to taste, and
  chopped

1 clove garlic, minced
½ teaspoon coriander
  (*cilantro*)
½ teaspoon oregano
Pinch dried ginger
6 eggs

Put the tomatoes in enough cold water to cover, and raise to a
boil. At once reduce heat to a simmer, and let cook ten minutes.
Heat the oil or lard in a heavy skillet and fry the onions.

Whip the chopped chiles to a pulp, and add to the transparent onions. Put in the garlic and seasonings and stir well. Hold a coarse sieve over the skillet, and push the drained tomatoes through it with a wooden spoon; this leaves the skins and seeds behind. Fold into a 6-egg omelet.

The next recipe comes from Mexico, but it used to be a favorite breakfast dish around Tucson and the Santa Cruz Valley. Despite its simplicity, it is remarkably tasty and different from anything you've ever eaten before.

TORTILLA CON BLANCOS
(*Tortilla with Eggs*)

3 tablespoons olive or	Salt
cooking oil	1 tortilla
2 eggs	

Heat the oil. Beat the eggs with a little salt until the whites and yolks are thoroughly blended.

Tear the tortilla into pieces about the size of a half dollar, and toss in the hot oil for a minute or less, not allowing them to turn darker than golden.

Add the eggs, and do not stir; tilt the pan from side to side and occasionally lift the cooked egg to allow the uncooked part to get into the oil.

Serve plain or with black pepper.

CHAPTER 7

Not all the country is dry

FISH RECIPES, BOTH FRESHWATER AND SALT

Two species of trout, several of catfish, probably some of the panfish of the sunfish genus, and even one eel are native to the Southwest. A great many other kinds of warm and cold water fish have been planted.

The Navajos, largest American tribe, have a strict taboo against eating fish, as do their cousins the Apaches and quite a few other Southwestern tribes. But the mountain Spanish are so fond of trout that one of their towns is named Truchas, and nearby Trampas means fish traps; while the Mexicans and their descendants, the Mexican-Americans, have a long and honored cuisine of sea and fresh water dishes.

Shrimps are from the Sea of Cortez, or Gulf of California, whichever you prefer. Many move into Arizona from Punto Peñasco, below Gila Bend, and Guaymas, below Nogales.

Before refrigeration brought shrimps to northern New Mexico, the people ate shrimp fritters, made from dried and powdered shrimps.

This is the traditional recipe. It can be improved by using fresh or canned or frozen shrimps, the tiniest size you can find; or larger shrimps cut up coarsely.

TORREJAS DE CAMARON
(*Shrimp Fritters*)

4 eggs	1 tablespoon dried chopped
4 ounces powdered shrimps	parsley
4 tablespoons white flour	Oil for deep frying
½ teaspoon baking powder	3 cups Sauce Number Four
2 teaspoons garlic salt	

Separate the eggs, beat the whites dry. Mix all the dry ingredients with the yolks, and add to the whites, folding in. Deep fry the batter in tablespoon-size fritters. Bring the Sauce Number Four to a simmer, drain the fritters in a slotted spoon, and drop into the simmering chile sauce.
Simmer for about twelve minutes.

Fresh shrimps are very good with green chile, but in this recipe, remove the seeds first; too much *picante* kills the flavor of the shellfish.

CAMARONES DE NOGALES
(*Shrimps from Nogales*)

2 pounds large shrimps	2 canned green chiles,
½ cup seasoned flour	seeded
1 cup peanut or soy oil	¾ cup dry sherry
	White rice

Shell and devein the shrimps, and roll them in flour. Let them stand while the oil gets as hot as possible; this is why peanut or soy oil is called for. Lay the shrimps in the oil, which should just cover them, and sauté for about five minutes. Remove the shrimps and keep warm; fry the chiles in the same oil. Put the shrimps back in with the chiles and start spooning the oil out. When you have gotten out as much as is feasible, pour the sherry in and serve at once on white rice.

A long time ago I rode fire patrol around a fishing lake and messed with the fire suppression crew, most of them Indians; I cooked supper every night. The sportsmen cleaned their fish into big cans, and I found out that they discarded roes along with the other innards. I sent the boys out to collect them after a big fishing day and cooked them this way:

HUEVAS INDIAS
(*Indian Roe*)

2 tablespoons fine-ground red chile	1 teaspoon salt
1 cup flour	2 pounds small fish roes (bass, bluegill, etc.)
1 teaspoon oregano	Cooking oil or lard

Mix the chile, flour, oregano, and salt thoroughly and roll the roes in the mixture. Let them stand at least ten minutes, preferably more, as this removes pockets of moisture from under the flour; if they are not removed, they will turn into steam and knock the crisp coating off.
Deep fry a few at a time in the oil or lard, and drain on brown paper.
Serve with a salad or boiled greens.

Dry salt cod should always be soaked overnight to get the salt out and the moisture back in.

Here are three Southwestern ways of cooking it, all delicious:

BACALAO NUEVO MEXICO
(New Mexican Salt Cod)

2 tablespoons cooking oil	1 teaspoon oregano
1 small onion in rings	1 pinch coriander (*cilantro*)
1 clove garlic, minced	1 pinch cumin (*comino*)
1 tortilla	1 ten-ounce can tomatoes
2 teaspoons fine-ground red	1 pound salt cod,
chile	pre-soaked

Cover the bottom of a heavy skillet with the oil, heat and render the onion rings soft. Add the garlic and cook slightly.
Tear the tortilla into tiny bits and fry quickly with the onion.
Mix the chile and herbs in the juice from the tomatoes, and return to tomatoes.
Break up the cod into bite-size pieces and put in an oiled casserole. Add the onion mixture and then the tomatoes and bake for an hour at 350° F.

BACALAO FRONTERIZO
(Border Style Salt Cod)

½ cup olive oil	1 tablespoon chopped fresh
1 pound codfish, pre-soaked	mint
1 large white onion, in	2 green chiles, fresh or
thick rings	canned
2 tablespoons piñon nuts	1½ pounds new potatoes,
1 pound ripe tomatoes,	unpeeled
peeled and sliced	

Heat the oil in a heavy skillet, and fry the cod about five minutes on each side. Then add the onion rings and the piñon nuts and cook another three or four minutes.

Mix the contents of the skillet and scrape into a buttered casserole. Put the tomatoes and mint into the skillet and simmer for five minutes.

Seed the chiles, roast and steam them if they are fresh, so as to pull the skin off. Cut the chiles into long, thin strips and cover the codfish mixture with them.

Gently pour the flavored tomatoes over all and bake at 350° F. for forty-five minutes.

Serve with small boiled potatoes.

Lamb's quarters, *quelites,* have other names in English: amaranth, pigweed, and white goosefoot. In the botanist's Latin, they are *Chenopodium album.*

Gathered wild in the spring, they are a great favorite with mountain people. They are sold dried in Santa Fe, and perhaps in the Mexican markets of such cities as New York, Chicago, or Los Angeles.

Spinach makes a good substitute; so, I imagine, would some of the greens so popular in the Southeast, such as mustard, kale, or collard.

QUELITES CON BACALAO
(*Cod with Greens*)

6 slices bacon	1 pound potatoes
½ cup flour	1 medium onion, finely
1 teaspoon freshly ground	chopped
black pepper	1 pound fresh lamb's
1 pound salt cod, pre-soaked	quarters (or spinach)

Try out the bacon in a heavy skillet; remove, drain, and crumble. Reserve the bacon.

Mix the flour and pepper; cut the cod into bite-size pieces and toss in the seasoned flour; reserve.

Peel and slice the potatoes and brown them lightly with the onion in the bacon fat. Turn the heat very low and allow the potatoes and onions to go on cooking lightly. Wash the lamb's quarters thoroughly and cook them in the water that clings to them.

Remove the potatoes and onions to a buttered casserole and fry the cod in the bacon fat. When almost done, remove with a slotted spoon and lay on the potatoes. Top with greens and a cup of the water in which they were cooked. Then lay the tried-out bacon on top of all, and bake for half an hour at 350° F.

Wherever the mountains rise into the Transition Zone, the streams are fast and cold; the states stock them with fine trout, native, German, rainbow, and so on. However, a few trout drift down into warm waters; in that case, they should be skinned before cooking.

TRUCHAS MONTESAS FRITAS
(*Fried Mountain Trout*)

1 cup flour	2 cups yellow cornmeal
2 teaspoons salt	2 cups cooking oil
1 teaspoon ground black pepper	¼ cup drawn butter
8 medium fresh trout	2 tablespoons lemon juice
2 eggs, beaten lightly	2 tablespoons chopped parsley

Mix the flour, salt, and pepper together thoroughly, and roll the trout in the mixture.

Then dip each fish in egg and finally in the cornmeal. Heat the

oil quite hot, but not smoking, in a heavy skillet and fry the fish, turning once.
Put the trout to drain and stay warm on brown paper, and mix the butter, lemon juice, and parsley together in a double boiler. Just before the mixture boils, transfer it to a sauce boat to be served alongside the trout.

TRUCHAS AZUL
(Blue Trout)

2 quarts salted water	2 sliced onions
1 cup vinegar	1 clove garlic, crushed
1 dried red chile	Large pinch thyme (*tomillo*)
2 *chilepequins or:*	2 large trout, cleaned
1 raw *jalapeño*	Lemon wedges
2 sliced carrots	Melted butter

Bring 2 quarts of salted water to a boil and add the vinegar, vegetables, and seasoning.
As soon as the liquid boils again, plunge the trout, one at a time so as not to lower the heat, into the pot. When both trout are at a boil, reduce the heat to a simmer and cook for about twenty minutes (more at high altitudes).
Serve with lemon wedges and melted butter.

TRUCHA RELLENA
(Stuffed Trout)

1 medium onion, chopped	1 teaspoon oregano
2 cloves garlic, minced	2 tortillas
Cooking oil	1 very large lake trout,
3 eggs	skinned and cleaned
1 ten-ounce can tomatoes	

Sauté the onion and garlic in the oil; beat the eggs and add them to the skillet, stirring slightly as they cook till almost firm. Whip in the tomatoes and oregano. Tear the tortillas fine, and mix them into the skillet. Stuff the trout with the mixture, which should be dry enough to handle, and place the fish in a buttered baking dish. Cover with aluminum foil, and bake at 350° F. for half an hour.

Almost every river in the Southwest is inhabited by catfish, at least in the lower reaches. William J. Koster, in his *Guide to the Fishes of New Mexico,* speaking of the bait used to catch cats, says: "Some are simple substances like chicken blood or cheese, and others are weird substances that resemble witches' brew both in the nature of their ingredients and in the secrecy with which the formula is guarded."

In my opinion, all catfish, including the finest channel cats, should be skinned before cooking. Let those who think otherwise go in peace.

After skinning, the fish can be cut crosswise in steaks about ¾ inch thick, or filleted. Catfish steaks are fine poached in Chile Caribe, Sauce Number Two.

Here is a more elaborate recipe:

BARBO VERDE
(*Green Catfish*)

¼ pound butter	1 bunch green onions
2 pounds catfish fillets	4 green tomatoes, medium
2 canned green chiles, seeded to reduce heat to taste	1 teaspoon oregano

Melt half the butter in a skillet. Put the fillets in the hot butter and brown one side.

Chop all the vegetables fine, and mix with the oregano.

Turn the fish, and dot the cooked side with the rest of the butter. Cover each fillet with the green vegetables and cover the skillet till the fish can be pierced with a table fork, about ten minutes.

The few natural lakes in the Southwest are almost all in very high country; but many, many dams have been built in this century, and these have all been stocked with the so-called pan or warm-water fishes.

The big wall-eye and the small yellow perch are particularly good. The wall-eye should be filleted, the yellow perch just split down the middle and the bones removed.

PERCA FRESCA
(*Fresh Perch*)

½ pound butter	½ cup piñon kernels
2 pounds wall-eye fillets *or:*	12 Spanish olives, stuffed
4 yellow perch, split	with pimentos
¼ cup blanched almonds, splintered	

Melt half the butter; brown one side of the fish in it. If the yellow perch are used, put the skin side down.

In a separate pan, bring the remaining butter to a boil; drop the nuts in and let them brown a little. Start spooning this mixture, always keeping it very hot, over the fish until the top side cooks, and a table fork will go all the way through the fish easily.

Garnish with the stuffed olives, sliced across, and serve.

✳   ✳   ✳

The sunfish family, chiefly the species called crappie, blue-gill, and bass, are the main catch of the Sunday boat renters on the reservoirs. They can be muddy tasting if the water is too warm; the best test is to put your elbow in the water. If it gets a shock, don't bother to skin your catch.

Unskinned, these panfish can be scaled and then treated like trout; skinned, like catfish.

Nopales are the joints of the beaver-tail cactus, *Opuntia tuna*. The fruit of the same cactus is sold as prickly pear, or made into candy or sometimes distilled into *tizwin*, which is the name for any alcoholic beverage in several Indian tongues.

Nopales can be bought in cans or jars in almost any Mexican food store, but if you have this book with you on a camping trip, put on heavy gloves, and with caution cut young leaves.

Well, they aren't really leaves, but let's not get technical: young beaver tails of the vegetable variety.

Lay the tails on a small bed of coals till the spines burn off. If you have been fishing, you will probably have pliers with you; if not, a cooking fork is handy for putting the nopales on the coals and turning them.

When cautious inspection shows that the spines are all gone, cut the joints up into 1-inch-square pieces and drop them into salted boiling water to cover. They will be done in about five to ten minutes, depending on the altitude.

Indoors, the spines can be burned away over a gas flame, and I have used a small blowtorch, though few kitchens are provided with this handy tool.

PESCADOS CON NOPALES
(*Fish and Cactus*)

½ cup cooking oil
1 whole clove garlic
1 teaspoon fine-ground chile
1 cup white flour
1½ pounds filleted fish
½ cup cooked or canned nopales

½ cup water in which nopales were canned or cooked
1 hard-cooked egg, sliced
1 teaspoon lemon juice
Salt

Heat the oil, fry the garlic in it. Discard the garlic. Mix the chile and flour and roll the fillets in the mixture. Fry in the garlicked oil until each side is slightly golden.

Then add the ½ cup water in which the nopales were canned, or boiled, and reduce the heat. Poach the fish until tender to a table fork. Put the nopales on top of the fish, and the sliced egg on top of the cactus. Sprinkle with a little lemon juice and salt.

PESCADO CON PAPAS
(*Fish with Potatoes*)

2 medium white potatoes, peeled and sliced
3 tablespoons lard or cooking oil
4 tablespoons butter
1 whole fish, about 3 pounds: panfish, lake trout, or Gulf of California catch

1 teaspoon oregano
Pinch thyme (*tomillo*)
Pinch marjoram (*mejorano*)
1 ten-ounce can tomatoes
1 large white onion, sliced thin
½ cup buttered bread crumbs
12 stuffed olives, sliced

Fry the potatoes in the lard or oil till quite brown.

Lightly butter a baking dish (or Dutch oven, if camping) and cover the bottom with the potatoes.

Lay the fish, cleaned and beheaded and scaled, if necessary, on the potatoes; sprinkle with herbs, and cover with the tomatoes and their juice.

Cover all with the onion slices, and dot them with the remaining butter. Sprinkle the bread crumbs evenly over all, garnish with the olive slices, and bake for half an hour at 450° F.

If cooking in an oven, remove the cover of the baking dish for the last five minutes; if in a Dutch oven, heap hot coals on the lid for the last ten minutes, in order to brown the bread crumbs.

Despite the centuries that most Spanish and Mexican people have been in the Southwest or in Mexico, the rice dishes of Old Spain have persisted. This last recipe for cooking fish is obviously derivative from the paella.

Olive oil gives this fish-and-rice dish a wonderful flavor, but it cannot be gotten as hot as soy or peanut oil; really hot oil improves the texture of the rice. Work out your own compromise.

If your diners are inclined to be late—a Southwestern trait —this dish can be held back by adding a little more water from time to time.

ARROZ CON PESCADO
(Fish with Rice)

½ cup cooking oil
2 small yellow or red
  onions, sliced
1 clove garlic, minced
1 cup rice, long grain or
  brown
2 pounds boned bass meat
3 cups boiling water
1 green chile, partly
  seeded and coarsely
  chopped

1 teaspoon coarse-ground
  red chile (*caribe*)
½ cup chopped parsley
Small pinch oregano
½ teaspoon saffron
2 cups fresh or frozen
  green peas

Put the oil in a heavy-bottomed pot that can be covered, get it quite hot and brown the onion and garlic. Take them out and put aside for the moment.

Put the rice in the hot oil, and stir steadily till each grain bursts a little.

Add the fish to the rice and return the onion and garlic. Stir for four or five minutes.

Add 3 cups boiling water and all the other ingredients. Cover, lower heat to a simmer, and cook thirty to forty minutes.

CHAPTER 8

Life starts with corn

TACOS, TAMALES, ENCHILADAS, AND

OTHER BASIC DISHES

The United States is a corn-eating, corn-based country. The pilgrims reported that they would have starved if they hadn't learned from the Indians how to plant maize, with a fish in each hill for fertilizer; and corn bread is still as familiar as codfish cakes to the New Englander.

The Middle West eats corn bread, too, and so does the South, which also insists on grits for breakfast. Pennsylvania's contribution is scrapple, and the Italian-Americans put polenta only second to pasta.

Here in the Southwest, amazingly, nothing very much like polenta is known; the nearest thing is an old New Mexican Spanish dish called *chauquehue,* a simple mixture of cornmeal —usually blue—and boiling water with a little fat and salt in it, a far cry from the meat- and cheese-filled mushes of Italy.

Our better corn dishes are largely of Mexican origin, based on something called *masa,* or Mexican dough.

Its manufacture resembles the Southern method of making grits, but the result is different.

It is no longer necessary to make your own *masa;* it never was if there was a Mexican bakery nearby. But the Quaker Oats people now make a sort of instant *masa* called Masa Harina, which is every bit as good as the Mexican product, though not quite up to the finest New Mexican blue corn, *masa azul.* So little blue corn is grown that this will never become an interstate item of commerce.

Below is the way to make *masa.* If you have been to Mexico or the Southwest, or just to Olvera Steet in Los Angeles, you may have bought yourself a *metate* and *mano,* the traditional Indian—Aztec, Pueblo, Papago, etc.—mortar and pestle.

If you have one, use it. A certain amount of the rock grinds off and gives an inimitable flavor. The old Spanish say that a man is not a man until he has eaten half a *metate,* and that it is his time to die when he has eaten two whole *metates.*

MASA
(Mexican Dough)

- **3 quarts cold water**
- **3 pounds fresh corn kernels**
- **3 ounces hydrated lime**

Put 3 quarts of cold water in a heavy kettle, and add the corn and lime. Heat to a boil and reduce the heat to a light bubbling that can be stopped by stirring.

Continue to cook until a sample kernel can be hulled between the fingers.

Remove, cool, drain, and hull with your hands. Rinse three times to get most, but not all, of the lime taste out; then grind on a *metate* or use a food mill if you must.

Making tortillas out of *masa* is not a recipe but a trick. Old ladies take a ball of *masa* in one hand and proceed to pat it round and thin between their palms; this is best done in pairs or larger groups, and accompanied by all the gossip of the town.

Young girls finish up by patting the tortilla against the bare thigh, just above the knee; fed to a young man, this will at once cause him to fall in love with the tortilla maker.

Moderns have tortilla presses, often very elaborate and expensive.

Whichever method is used, the flat disk is then finished in a heavy iron skillet which has been prepared with a mixture of slaked lime and water, half and half, heated a few minutes and poured out. The skillet is then wiped with a clean cloth, and the tortilla baked a minute to each side.

Or buy fresh, frozen, or canned tortillas, depending on where you are.

Tortillas de Harina are made with ordinary white flour, and can be pretty good, but they are no substitute for real tortillas, except as noted below.

TORTILLAS DE HARINA
(*Flour Tortillas*)

6 tablespoons lard	1 cup lukewarm water plus
4 cups flour,	additional water
sifted with:	
2 teaspoons salt	

Work the lard into the flour with your fingers and knead thoroughly. Then work in a cup of lukewarm water and keep adding more water, a spoon at a time, till the dough comes clear of the sides of the bowl. Separate the dough into balls the size of a large egg, and put them in the refrigerator for at least fifteen minutes, perhaps more. Then roll them out on a floured board with a floured pin until they are very thin and about six inches in diameter.

Heat a very heavy iron skillet or griddle very hot, and cook the tortillas two minutes on one side and a minute on the other.

These are very good eaten instead of bread or corn tortillas, especially if the entrée is a *masa* dish such as enchiladas or Tamales or Tamale Pie. They are the only wrapping ever used in a Santa Fe *burrito*. Tradition says that the name of this tidbit comes from an old Spanish saying: "If I had a horse, I would go make my fortune, but I have only a little burro," little burro being *burrito,* of course.

In other words, "If I had meat, I'd dine well, but I have only some leftover beans."

BURRITOS

8 Flour Tortillas	1 cup mashed potatoes
2 cups cooked, unfried beans	2 green chiles, chopped
	Salt

Warm the tortillas slightly. Mix the beans, potatoes, and chiles thoroughly, and salt to taste.

Divide the mixture into eighths and roll in the warm tortilla.

I have heard of *burritos* being filled with all kinds of things, including pork cracklings, and a cup or so of Sauce Number Five or Sauce Number Eight can be used instead of the straight green chile. Sometimes you get cheese in your *bur-*

rito; in other words, as the name implies, a *burrito* is filled with whatever you have. But always some beans go into the filling.

Of course, *burritos* must be eaten with the fingers.

In the upper Santa Cruz Valley, between Tucson and Nogales, they pat or roll flour tortillas until they are 12 to 18 inches in diameter; it is easy to read large type through them.

Then they make *burritos* as above, first folding down the top and bottom of the tortilla to add strength.

These are then deep-fried, and called Chimichangos, a word with absolutely no meaning in any Indian or Spanish dialect that anyone ever heard of. The translation might be "thingumajigs," but the flavor is delicious.

Back to the corn tortillas: lightly fried in oil or lard, they become Tostados, which can be broken up and served with cocktails.

Filled with a meat or cheese mixture or both, folded in two and fried crisp, they become tacos; rolled around (Arizona) or alternately stacked with (New Mexico) various savory mixtures, they become enchiladas.

The line between enchiladas and tacos is not too clear. Mexicans from the central valley of the Republica call things tacos that I would call enchiladas, and sometimes the nomenclature runs the other way around. My rule, and the one that prevails all over the Southwest and the border is that the enchilada is cooked in an oven and under a moist sauce, and the taco is finished in the skillet, with its tortilla left crisp.

Tacos should always be served with shredded lettuce, grated cheese, and sliced or chopped raw onions on the side. Each person adds one, all, or none of these to his taco filling just before eating. Also, tacos should be served with two paper napkins per each. And, preferably, you should stroll and listen to Mexican music while doing the eating, but that isn't always possible in a small apartment.

TACOS DE GALLINA
(*Chicken Tacos*)

1 three-pound hen
Boiling water
2 cloves garlic
1 teaspoon black pepper
1 tablespoon coriander
  (*cilantro*)
Salt
1 large onion, minced

2 tablespoons lard or
  cooking oil
1 four-ounce can tomato
  paste
1 four-ounce can chopped
  green chiles
1 teaspoon oregano
8 tortillas

Cover the hen with boiling water, add the cloves of garlic, black
pepper, coriander, and salt; bring to a boil again. Reduce to a

simmer and cook till experiment tells you that you can slip the
meat off the fowl easily; but stop before the meat falls off by
itself.

Skin the hen and return the skin and bones to the soup to make
broth for another occasion. (If you were Mexican, you would
serve it at the very end of the evening, just before your guests
went home or your family retired.)

Meanwhile, fry the onion quite brown in ¾ of the lard and
add the garlic minced and crushed with the wooden handle of
your knife. Stop the frying with the tomato paste and add the
chopped chiles and the oregano. Dilute to a thick sauce with
a little chicken broth, and put in the boned chicken meat.

Put a little oil or lard in a heavy skillet, and lay a tortilla in it.
As soon as the hot grease has softened the tortilla, put 2 kitchen
spoons of the sauce in, fold in half. Keep very hot and repeat

with the other 7 tortillas, dividing up any remaining sauce at the very end. Eat at once. These cannot be kept warm until needed.

The method of making tacos doesn't vary, only the fillings do. Here are some more:

TACOS DE CARNE
(*Beef Tacos*)

2 pounds lean chuck round steak	1 teaspoon coriander (*cilantro*)
½ cup oil or lard	½ cup lukewarm water
1 large onion, minced	2 tablespoons coarse-ground
1 clove garlic, minced	chile (*chile caribe*)
½ teaspoon cumin (*comino*) seeds	

Chop the meat up into ¼-inch cubes and brown in the oil or lard with the onion and garlic. Season with the herbs, crushing the cumin first on a wet chopping board. Add ½ cup of lukewarm water, and slowly stir in the chile. When the mixture thickens, it is ready to be made into tacos, as in Tacos de Gallina, above.

TACOS DE PUERCO ADOVADO
(*Tacos with Marinated Pork*)

2 pounds lean pork	6 teaspoons fine-ground red chile
1 cup orange juice	½ teaspoon coriander (*cilantro*)
1 tablespoon lemon juice	⅛ pound (¼ cup) butter
1 cup tomato juice	

Cut the pork into ¼-inch cubes and marinate in a mixture of all the other ingredients for at least four hours, preferably much longer. Take the pork out of the mixture and bake in a slow oven, about 300° F. for an hour. If it seems to be drying out too much, add some butter. Meanwhile, simmer marinade down to half its bulk. Return roasted pork, simmer for a few minutes, and make into tacos, as in Tacos de Gallina.

The next taco mixture is completely untraditional. But it is in the Moorish tradition of Spain, a feeble excuse for tampering with something as sacred as a taco.

A stronger excuse is that it is delicious.

TACOS CON BERENJENA
(Tacos with Eggplant)

1 large eggplant	2 tablespoons lard or
6 ounces cream cheese	cooking oil
1 large red onion, chopped	2 cups Sauce Number One
½ pound hamburger	

Boil the eggplant till done; peel and chop very fine. Warm the cream cheese to room temperature and whip it into the eggplant pulp.

Fry the onion and then the hamburger, breaking up the latter with a fork. When the onion is transparent and the meat brown, mix them into the cheese-eggplant mixture, thoroughly. Make into tacos. Just before serving, spoon a generous portion of Sauce Number One into each.

The cheese and eggplant make a wonderfully bland contrast to the hot sauce. Most Spanish or Mexican restaurants offer two kinds of enchiladas, red and green. Sometimes—horrors—the green enchiladas have nothing in them but canned mushroom soup, canned green chiles, and perhaps a little cheese. This sort of thing, if it continues, would justify giving the country back to the Indians who, while often not very good cooks, wouldn't do *that.*

ENCHILADAS DE POLLO
(*Chicken Enchiladas*)

2 pounds chicken breasts, fresh or frozen
2 medium onions, cut in rings
1 clove garlic
1 stalk celery
½ pint sour cream
½ pound sharp club Cheddar cheese
½ cup peanut oil
1 ten-ounce can tomatoes
1 four-ounce can chopped green chiles
Pinch coriander (*cilantro*)
Pinch oregano
12 tortillas

Simmer the chicken breasts in water to cover with 1 onion, the garlic, and the celery until the meat is ready to slip off the bones. Return the bones to the soup, and cook down to 1 cup.

Shred the chicken and mix with the sour cream and cheese; if you use the club type, breaking up with a kitchen fork is enough, otherwise grate the cheese coarsely.

In a heavy saucepan fry the second onion in ¾ of the oil till transparent; add the tomatoes, chiles, chicken broth, and herbs, and simmer down by about a fourth.

Put the saucepot on the right-hand front burner of the stove; place a small heavy skillet, with the rest of the oil in the bottom, on the left-hand burner. Heat the oil quite hot, but not smoking.

(Of course, left-handers may find that reversing the position will make things easier.)

Take a pancake turner and slide a tortilla into the oil; when the tortilla blisters, or balloons, slip it out again and let the oil drain back. Dip the tortilla into the simmering sauce, take it out at once, and place it in a baking dish.

Fill the tortilla with the sour cream-chicken-cheese mixture and fold it over.

Repeat till all 12 tortillas are filled.

Place the baking dish in the oven. All this can be done well in advance.

Forty minutes before mealtime, place tortillas in oven preheated to about 250° F. Twenty minutes later, raise the heat to 350° F. and pour the sauce over the enchiladas.

The red chile enchilada recipe I have picked is New Mexican. In Arizona—and along the southern border of New Mexico—it would probably be served with the tortillas folded over the filling, and the fried egg would be omitted. Raw chopped onions and a bowl of *Salsa Picante* (Sauce Number One) are always put on the table with these enchiladas, and sometimes freshly chopped mint is passed, too. Sauces Number Six or Seven can be used instead of Number One on the table; Sauce Number Two is used in the cooking.

ENCHILADAS COLORADAS
(Red Chile Enchiladas)

½ cup cooking oil	1 ⚹300 can pitted ripe
1 large onion, chopped	olives
2 cloves garlic, minced	12 tortillas
2 cups Sauce Number Two	4 fresh eggs
¾ pound grated or cumbled Cheddar cheese	

This dish is best cooked in two skillets, one a little deeper than the other, and each about 7 inches in diameter; but the deeper one can be a shallow saucepan if it heavy enough in gauge. In the deeper pan, fry the onion and garlic in the ½ cup oil till tender. Then add the sauce, stir well and bring to simmer. Place this on the right-hand front burner of your stove, and put the shallow skillet on the left-hand burner with enough oil or lard to cover the bottom about an inch deep. On a table to the right of the stove—your right, as you face it—put out four dinner plates, the bowl of crumbled cheese, and the olives, each cut in two crossways. Left-handers may prefer the reverse order. Set your oven to preheat at 200° F., and you are ready. Dip each tortilla in the hot oil, let the oil drain back into the skillet, then dip the tortilla for a full thirty seconds in the simmering sauce. Lay the tortilla on the first plate, cover it with cheese, and sprinkle olives over it. Repeat for the second plate, and so on, then add a second layer to each plate, identical with the first. For the third layer, just fry your tortilla; the sauce should have been used up by now. If not, divide it among the four plates on top of the cheese, just before you put the olives on. Put the four plates in the oven and carefully fry 4 eggs, sunny-side up, basting with the hot oil or lard in which the tortillas were softened until whites are done. Put an egg on each stack of enchiladas and serve as soon as the cheese melts and starts running out the edge of the tortilla, all of which is a lot easier than it sounds.

In order to rise above a charge of discrimination and provincialism, the green chile recipe below is given for folded, or rolled, tortillas. To serve it in the manner of the Sangre de Cristo Mountains, start with a flat fried tortilla, spoon the chile sauce over it, crumble the cheese on that, repeat once, top with a plain fried tortilla and crown with a fried egg.

ENCHILADAS VERDES
(*Green Enchiladas*)

1 teaspoon fine-ground red chile	4 tablespoons flour
1 four-ounce can green chiles, seeded and chopped	4 tablespoons butter
	2 tablespoons oil or lard
	8 tortillas
	½ pound Cheddar cheese,
1 teaspoon oregano	grated or crumbled
4 cups very strong chicken broth	

Simmer the red and green chile and oregano in the chicken broth till it is reduced to 3 cups. Make a roux of the flour and butter, and slowly work it into the chicken-chile mixture until it is smooth. Set this mixture to keep warm.

Heat an inch of oil or lard in a small skillet, and dip a tortilla in it quickly, let the oil drain back, and lay the tortilla in a baking dish. Spoon the chicken-chile sauce into it, add cheese and fold the tortilla in half, or lay the mixture, cheese-topped, in the middle, and fold both edges of the tortilla in to make a roll.

Repeat until all the tortillas are in the baking dish and filled; then bake at 350° F. for about fifteen minutes.

Now comes the tamale, which is much easier than it looks. You will need corn husks, but these are really no problem; the green leaves of table corn—sweet corn in the East; roastin' ears in the Middle West and South—can be laid in a sunny windowsill, where they will dry perfectly; then they can be stored almost indefinitely.

Here in the Southwest we buy our corn husks, because you can get much larger ones from field corn than you can from table corn. The small tamales, however, are just as good as the big ones; you just eat more of them.

We use Masa Harina, but if there is a Mexican bakery nearby, you could buy your *masa* ready-mixed. I don't want to give directions for mixing Masa Harina, since they will be on the package, and it is possible that the manufacturers will change them from time to time.

TAMALES

1½ pounds lean, boneless pork	4 cups Sauce Number One, Five, or Seven
Salt	Dried corn husks
4 cloves garlic	4 (approximately) cups *masa*

Cut the pork into 1-inch cubes, cover with salted water, add the garlic, peeled, but whole, and simmer till quite tender. Remove the garlic and discard. Drop the pork into the chile sauce, bring to a boil and cook down till it makes a fairly thick paste. Cool this mixture.

Lay corn husks out in stacks, two or three husks thick, and coat with *masa,* about ⅛ inch thick. Spoon the chile-pork paste on one edge, but leave at least 2 inches at each end of the husks for your tie-up. Fold the loaded edge of the husks toward the center and continue folding to the middle; then just roll the rest of the way.

Fold each empty end in half and tie with a twist of split corn husk.

Place the tied tamales in a metal colander and place in a pot filled with water not quite high enough to touch the bottom of the colander.

Steam for forty-five minutes to an hour in a covered pot.

Tamales are now ready to eat, but they can be frozen and reheated, with or without steam.

Tamales can be made of almost any kind of meat. The chicken tamale is very popular; beef, mutton, lamb, or turkey are all good. Veal has a tendency to disappear, as does very young chicken.

San Francisco, in gold rush days, had a scandal about tamales; the most popular tamale maker in town was exposed as using seagulls in his chicken tamales.

There is a sweet tamale, made with raisins and corn syrup or molasses, but I do not favor it.

Tamale Pie, I am pretty sure, is a California invention; the fact that ripe olives are always used in it makes pretty strong evidence. But it long since spread into the Southwest as a favorite dish.

I like dark meat of turkey in a Tamale Pie, and markets frequently sell turkey legs all by themselves. But pork, round or flank steak of beef, leg of mutton, and even wild pigeon make wonderful pies. Some use hamburger, but I don't approve.

TAMAL EN CACEROL
(*Tamale Pie*)

1½ pounds meat	1 cup beef consommé
2 tablespoons oil or lard	(canned will do)
2 cups Sauce Number Two	8 cups *masa*
or Seven	¼ pound grated sharp
1 large onion, chopped	Cheddar cheese
1 ╳303 can pitted	
black olives	

Cut the meat into ½-inch cubes, and brown in oil or lard. Reduce heat and cook for ten minutes. Remove the meat and simmer in the chile sauce. In the oil, render the onion soft, and add to the mixture, together with the olives and the consommé. Butter a 2-quart casserole, and line it with three-quarters of the *masa*. Pour in the meat-chile mixture and top with the remaining *masa*.

Sprinkle the cheese over the top evenly, and bake at 350° F. for forty-five minutes.

CHAPTER 9

Meat makes the carnival

KID, LAMB, MUTTON, BEEF, AND PORK

The Spanish spell it *carnaval,* and meat is *carne;* until I looked it up, I thought that any time an old-time family had meat on the table, it was a carnival.

Actually, the word was originally confined to the pre-Lenten feast, and means the taking away of meat.

No matter. It was not so long ago that many a ranch and many a village had no refrigeration at all, and when an animal was slaughtered, a pretty gay time was at hand.

Nowadays, the Rural Electrification program reaches most everyone, and those it doesn't have refrigerators run by kerosene or bottled gas. Future generations will never know the fun of driving several miles through the mountains with a cake of ice on a bumper of the car; in fact, today's bumpers wouldn't accommodate a 50-pound chunk.

Cabrito, baby kid, and *borrego,* suckling lamb, are great favorites among the Spanish and Mexican-Americans. In Mexico proper, they seem to manage to have *cabrito* all year round, and when a restaurant hangs out a sign advertising the delicacy, the noise of squealing brakes is loud in the land, as cars stop abruptly and back up.

The little animals weigh from 2½ pounds up to 10 pounds. As explained in Chapter 5, in traditional Southwest butchering the backbone is removed intact, then the animal is quartered. The blood and intestines are made into pudding, the head into a very delicate brawn; the ribs, if the weight is over 5 pounds, are put aside for separate roasting in a mild barbecue sauce; and the hindquarters and shoulders are roasted.

You will need at least 1½ pounds of meat per person, which may sound like a lot; but be assured that there will be no leftovers, to the host's regret.

The recipe for *cabrito* can be used for *borrego,* and vice versa. In the Sangre de Cristos and south into Santa Fe, an herb called *chimaja* would be used instead of the fennel, but I doubt if it can be obtained even in Albuquerque.

CABRITO ASADO
(*Roast Kid*)

1 tablespoon powdered fennel	8 strips bacon
	4 cloves garlic
1 teaspoon fine-ground red chile	6 pounds suckling kid, shoulder or hindquarters
Salt	1 quart water

Mix the fennel, chile, and ample salt together. Cut up 4 of the strips of bacon into pieces about an inch long. Peel the garlic cloves, and slit them into long, narrow strips; fold each in a piece of the cut-up bacon, and insert each package into a slit cut in the meat, getting the bacon as close to the bone as possible.

Rub the meat with the salt and spice mixture and place on a baking rack over a pan containing about a quart of water. Lay a bacon strip over each piece of meat.

Bake at 450° F. for half an hour; then lower the heat to 300° F., and bake another hour, basting frequently with the water and drippings from the pan. Skim the water-drippings and serve with the meat. If necessary, boil the gravy down a little, but do not thicken with flour.

Never serve Sauce Number One with *cabrito,* but a little mint jelly goes very well. Either French bread or mashed potatoes should be provided to take up the clear gravy.

BORREGO AL HORNO
(*Lamb in the Oven*)

½ teaspoon fine-ground red chile	1 clove garlic, minced
1 teaspoon dried mint	2 tablespoons oil, preferably olive
1 teaspoon thyme (*tomillo*)	5 pounds suckling lamb

Mix the chile, herbs, and garlic into the oil, and rub every surface of the lamb thoroughly. Bake on a rack over a quart of water, very slowly, at 300° F. or even slightly less.

The gravy, skimmed, can be thickened with flour and butter, but it is fine served clear in individual cups, with French bread to dip.

The next two recipes may have more historical than culinary value. Even if you can persuade a Spanish, Mexican, or Italian butcher to sell you the roasting meat from a little kid

or lamb, he probably will save the pluck for his own family.
But if you're lucky, here is how the mountain people make:

MORCILLA DE CABRITO
(*Kid's Blood Pudding*)

2 cups small intestines
2 cups honeycomb tripe
1 quart kid's blood
2 tablespoons lard
1 medium onion, cut in
   rings

2 cloves garlic, chopped
1 teaspoon oregano
1 teaspoon dried mint
1 first or second stomach

All the meat must be from a very young kid. Cut the intestines
and tripe up into 1-inch-square or -long pieces, and fry with the
blood in lard. Add the onion and garlic, and keep stirring constantly until a bit of the small intestine is tender to the bite.
Add the herbs and cook slowly for another five minutes.
Stuff into the first (or second) stomach. (The tripe is from
the third stomach.) Sew shut, and place in a colander or
cheesecloth bag, and suspend over steam for two hours.

CABEZITA
(*Little Head*)

1 head *borrego* (suckling
   lamb) or *cabrito* (baby
   kid)
1 large onion, whole
1 clove garlic, whole
1 teaspoon fine-ground red
   chile
1 teaspoon thyme
   (*tomillo*)

1 teaspoon oregano
1 teaspoon sage
1 teaspoon cloves
1 teaspoon powdered
   mustard
4 tablespoons vinegar

Split the head and put in a kettle with enough water to cover. Bring to a boil twice, and skim carefully each time. Reduce to a simmer, and add all the other ingredients. In about three hours, the meat will start to fall off the bones.
Turn off the heat and allow the head to cool in the water. Discard the onion and garlic. Then remove all the meat carefully, skin the tongue, and cut everything edible into ¼-inch cubes. Pack tightly into a bowl and chill for at least three days.
Slice and eat with *Salsa Picante* (Sauce Number One).

You may have more luck getting the ribs of a *cabrito* or *borrego*. They will not make a meal, but served with plenty of beans, they are more than a good meal.
Eat the ribs first, with your fingers, and then fill up on beans, cooked in any of the manners described in their chapter.
No weight is given for the ribs; get as many as you can.

ASADITO
(*Little Roast*)

4 large tomatoes	2 tablespoons vinegar
1 four-ounce can green chiles	Ribs suckling lamb or kid
2 tablespoons brown sugar	2 cups water
2 teaspoons dried thyme (*tomillo*)	

Carefully scoop the centers out of the tomatoes and reserve the cores. Divide the chiles, seeds and all, into four portions and place one part in each tomato.
Put the tomatoes in a baking dish and add water to cover them halfway up. Bake at 300° F. for half an hour.

Let the tomatoes cool and remove and discard the chiles. Pulp the tomatoes with their cores, and add all the other ingredients, except water, stirring vigorously. Marinate the ribs in this mixture for eight hours. Then remove the ribs and start the marinade simmering, adding 2 cups of water and then cooking down till 1 cup has evaporated. Lay the ribs on a roasting rack over a pan containing the marinade. Roast at 300° F., basting constantly, until the sauce has cooked down to where most of it clings to the ribs. Eat at once.

The chile flavors the tomatoes just enough to give a *picante* aftertaste; while actually chewing the meat off the tiny bones, it isn't apparent.

The riblets of older lamb, called lamb breast by butchers, are terribly fat; the best way to cook them is to simmer them in Sauce Number Two for an hour or more; then cool the sauce, skim thoroughly, bake the ribs for fifteen minutes at 350° F. and serve with sauce hot over rice.

Spareribs of pork and short ribs of beef are fine subjects for barbecuing. It is usually thought, both in and out of the Southwest, that barbecuing originated here, or at least in Mexico; but the word comes from the Caribbean, where the beardless Indians observed bearded sailors coming ashore to shoot game and roast it in a ground pit. *Barba* is Spanish for beard, and *barbacoa* is Mexican-Spanish for barbecue.

When you help a rancher slaughter a steer or a cow, he always gives you meat to take home. Since the country I spent most of my riding days in raised grassers almost exclusively—grazed animals that then went to stockyards to be finished off on corn or cottonseed cake—and since slaughtering is almost always done when there hasn't been rain for a long time, and the grass is dry and growing sparse, steaks and chops were inclined to be tough; but living on dry grass improves the short ribs, if anything, and cooked cowboy style, are exceptionally good if served with a salad, and the Palomar-style Beans as listed in the Index; but the beans and ribs together may be too much for an indoor meal.

Technically speaking, this rib dish isn't a barbecue, since it's done in a skillet or Dutch oven.

COSTILLAS FALSAS ESTILO VAQUERO
(*Cowboy Short Ribs*)

4 pounds short ribs	½ teaspoon ground nutmeg
2 tablespoons oil or lard	1 teaspoon black pepper
1 large onion, cut in rings	1 bottle light beer
1 clove garlic, minced	1 pound tomatoes
½ cup white flour	2 tablespoons soy sauce
2 tablespoons coarse-ground chile (*chile caribe*)	

Cut the short ribs into 1-inch lengths and brown in oil in a dry, heavy skillet. Remove and allow to cool. Brown the onion and garlic in the oil or lard.

Toss the browned ribs in the flour and put them, and any remaining flour, back in the skillet with the onion and garlic. Turn and toss the ribs until the flour is browned.

Make a paste of the chile, nutmeg, and black pepper with a little of the beer.

Put the tomatoes into the skillet, and as they warm, crush them with a wooden spoon and thicken the juice with the chile paste. Then add the rest of the beer and the soy sauce; reduce heat to a boil so gentle that it can be stopped by stirring, and cook the ribs in the sauce for an hour or more.

The sparerib recipe below is a real barbecue, but it will
work pretty well under the broiler of a gas or electric oven:

COSTILLAS DE PUERCO
(*Spareribs*)

4 **pounds spareribs, in racks**	2 **tablespoons fresh ground**
4 **cloves garlic, whole**	**ginger** *or:*
1 **tablespoon cornstarch**	1 **teaspoon dried**
1 **ten-ounce can pineapple**	**ginger** *and*
rings	1 **teaspoon fresh**
2 **tablespoons soy sauce**	**horseradish**
2 **teaspoons vinegar**	1 **teaspoon cumin** (*comino*)
2 *chilepequins* **(bird peppers)**	

Rub the spareribs vigorously with the garlic. Mix the cornstarch
to a smooth paste with a little water, and put in a saucepan
with the juice from the pineapple. Warm slowly, stirring, and
gradually add the soy sauce and the vinegar.

Crush the *chilepequins* and add them and the ginger (or its
substitute) and the cumin to the sauce. Raise the heat a little
till you get a bubble, and stir until the sauce is about as thick
as ketchup.

Put the ribs about six inches above or below charcoal coals or
a broiler, and paint the exposed side with the sauce. Repeat in
five minutes.

After ten minutes, turn the ribs and paint the second side. If
you are broiling *under* a broiler, at this time put the pineapple
rings on the ribs and paint both the rings and the ribs with
the sauce.

The ribs are done after ten minutes a side under a broiler;
but if you are cooking *over* coals, turn them a second time, and
now put the pineapple on top and paint a final time; allow to
broil for another five minutes.

Serve with sauerkraut or baked squash.

Mutton is the native meat of northern New Mexico, and, to some extent, northern Arizona, too; lamb is fiesta meat. The Lower Sonoran is beef country, but, alas, not beef finishing country; the cowboy ate his steak pounded, floured, and called chicken-fried steak. The *vaquero* stewed his beef with chile in a variety of ways.

Nowadays, fine beef comes into the country from Omaha and Kansas City, and perhaps even from the cottonseed cake feeders in Los Angeles, and Anglo-style steaks are universally enjoyed. But elderly Mexican-Americans, *los viejos*, still insist that meat is better cut the Mexican way, with the grain instead of across it. It does keep the juices in, and if you can get your butcher to cut a chunk of beef or lamb loin this way, try grilling it and then slicing thin before serving.

Since this is written in sight of the Sangre de Cristos, where sheep is still king (queen?), mutton comes first, then beef, and finally pork, which is a little more Mexican than New Mexican.

You can use lamb in any mutton recipe, cutting down the cooking time according to the grade. Genuine spring lamb, according to government regulations, is always less than five months old; spring lamb less than twelve; past that age the meat is sold as yearling lamb, or yearling mutton, retailer's choice.

PUCHERO
(*Boiled Dish*)

2 pounds lean, boneless mutton loin	1 large can tomatoes
1 small bunch beets with tops	2 sour cooking apples, whole
1 head cabbage, whole	1 large dried chile (red)
6 large carrots, whole	1 tablespoon oregano
4 large white onions	Pinch dried mint
1 bunch turnips with tops	Pinch ground cloves (*clavas*)
	Pinch ground cinnamon

Wash all the vegetables thoroughly; do not peel the beets.
Put the meat in a heavy kettle, cover with cold water, bring
to a boil and skim, twice. Add everything else, bring to a boil
again, then reduce to a simmer and cook two to three hours,
depending on altitude. Remove the meat and place in the center
of a large platter. Fish out turnips and beets, cut off the tubers
and peel.
Mix the beet and turnip roots and pile at one end of the meat
platter. Mix the green tops and pile at other end. Cut the
cabbage into wedges and place on either side of the meat.
Alternate the other vegetables around the meat, and serve, carving
at the table.

Unlike the other recipes in this chapter, the next one is
not for four; a leg of lamb or, particularly, a leg of mutton
feeds more people than that. But what is nicer than leftover lamb in the refrigerator?

PIERNA DE CARNERO
(*Leg of Lamb*)

2 cloves garlic	¼ teaspoon dried ground
4 tablespoons blanched	ginger
almonds	1 teaspoon ground cloves
2 tablespoons olive oil	(*clavas*)
Juice ½ lemon	1 leg of lamb
1 teaspoon fine-ground red	1 cup sherry
chile	1 cup dry red wine

Put the garlic and almonds in a mortar, and pound to a paste.
Gradually add the oil, stirring always in the same direction, till
a mayonnaise consistency is achieved. Then stir in the lemon
juice, chile, ginger, and cloves.
Pierce the lamb all over with a sharp knife, and while the knife

holds the hole open fill with the paste. Be sure to get some of the paste against the bone that shows at the bottom end of the leg. Mix the two wines, and pour over the meat in a glass or ceramic dish. Allow to stand overnight, or longer, spooning the wine up over the meat when you think of it.

Roast at 350° F., twenty minutes per pound for leg of lamb, thirty minutes for mutton.

CHULETAS DE CARNERO SABROSAS
(*Savory Lamb Chops*)

8 thick lamb rib chops *or:*	**4 medium green tomatoes,**
4 thick shoulder chops	**peeled**
¼ pound smoked ham,	**½ teaspoon saffron**
preferably country style	**1 teaspoon fine-ground red**
1 large yellow onion,	**chile**
chopped	**1 teaspoon dried oregano**
1 clove garlic, minced	**Pinch cumin** (*comino*)
	Pinch coriander (*cilantro*)

Brown both sides of the chops, remove from the skillet and keep warm. Cut the ham into small pieces and brown in the same skillet the chops were done in. As the ham tries out, add the onion and garlic and stir till they are soft and a little brown. Then put in the tomatoes, quartered, and as they cook, pulp them with a cooking spoon.

Take out a couple of large spoonfuls of the juice and allow to cool, so as to dissolve the saffron. While the juice is cooling, add the chile and herbs and the spices, and stir slowly, over a fairly high heat. Replace the saffron and fluid when possible. As soon as the sauce is reduced to the consistency of a watery ketchup, put the lamb chops back in the pan and carefully spoon sauce over them.

Cover the pan and cook at a simmer for twenty to thirty minutes. The chops should show the very faintest sign of pinkness in the middle when they are done.

CHULETAS DE CARNERO CON PIÑONES
(Lamp Chops with Piñon Nuts)

4 tablespoons piñon kernels, roasted	¾ cup olive oil
3 cloves garlic	¼ cup cider vinegar
1 tablespoon coarse-ground red chile (*caribe*)	3 pounds lamb or mutton chops, cut into four portions
1 can tomato paste	

Grind the piñon kernels in a mortar with the garlic and chile, until they are an oily blend. Whip in the tomato paste, and slowly add the oil, as in mayonnaise. When done, add the vinegar, with a little less care. (Or put all in an electric blender for five minutes.)

Paint both sides of the chops with the sauce and grill over a charcoal bed, or under a broiler. Place about 6 inches from the heat.

Every five minutes, turn the chops and repaint the exposed surface.

The chops will be done in half an hour.

Prime rib of beef is not a Southwestern dish; Texans who have moved West like it well done, which is a crime, and the Spanish and Mexicans are still at the steak stage, largely.

But the best prime ribs I have ever eaten were found in Yuma, Arizona, where Dick Crossley, who runs the Charcoal House, told me that he rubbed his roast with rock salt before putting it in the oven.

I have never tried this, but I have found that making a paste of table salt works fine. The paste promptly bakes into a solid cake and keeps all the juices in without allowing the salt to penetrate the meat.

As already mentioned, bunkhouse cooks chicken-fry their steaks. Then they make white gravy of flour and water. No further mention is necessary.

The Spanish, when they get a tough steak, cut it about 2 inches thick and cook it as follows:

CARNE SANTA FE
(*Santa Fe Steak*)

1 cup flour
1½ pounds round or
  boneless chuck steak
2 tablespoons oil or lard
1 four-ounce can green
  chiles, chopped
1 teaspoon dried mint
  leaves

1 medium red onion
1 ten-ounce can tomatoes
1 teaspoon brown sugar
½ teaspoon dried fennel
2 cups water *or:*
  1 cup water and 1 cup
  dry Red wine

Pound the flour into the steak with the edge of a saucer; keep this up till all the flour has been used up.

Heat oil or lard in a heavy skillet or Dutch oven, and brown all sides and edges of the steak.

Add everything else, with 2 cups of water (or 1 cup of water and 1 cup of dry red wine).

Cover, reduce heat to a simmer, and cook for an hour and a half.

The preceding dish is from the very north of the Southwest. Down on the border, they do it a little differently.

CARNE ESTILO NOGALES
(*Nogales-style Steak*)

2 pounds round or rump steak, 2 inches thick	1 teaspoon oregano
1 large yellow onion, chopped	2 tablespoons flour
2 cloves garlic, minced	1 cup tomato sauce
1 green chile, peeled, with most of the seeds removed	½ bottle light beer
	2 tablespoons dry sherry

Remove any fat from the meat and rub the fat all over the inside of a heavy skillet, which is warming while you work.
Raise the heat in the skillet till the fat begins to smoke a little, and brown the meat on both sides. Remove the meat, put the vegetables in the skillet, cover them with the meat and sprinkle the oregano and flour all over the exposed surface of the steak; then turn the steak flour side down, and add the tomato sauce and beer.
Cover tightly and reduce the heat to a simmer; cook about two hours and add the sherry just before serving.

The next dish is usually eaten alone, but it also makes an unusual filling for tacos. Any kind of leftover meat will work.

PICADILLO
(*Spanish Hash*)

1 yellow onion, medium-sized, chopped	4 ounces soup stock or canned bouillon
2 tablespoons oil	¼ cup seeded raisins or currants
3 cups cooked meat, chopped or put through a coarse grinder once	½ teaspoon coriander (*cilantro*)
2 medium ripe tomatoes, peeled and quartered	Pinch ground cloves (*clavas*)

Fry the onion soft, then add the meat, stirring vigorously; when the meat is browned, add the tomatoes and mix all thoroughly with a wooden spoon. Add the broth, raisins, and seasonings, and bring to a boil; cover and reduce heat to a simmer; cook about half an hour.

The next recipe was stolen by me from the Fred Harvey restaurant in Gallup, almost thirty years ago. Over the years it has probably changed somewhat; recipes have a habit of doing this.

PICADILLO DE CARNE SALMUERADO
(*Corned Beef Hash*)

1 pound corned beef, canned or not	2 large white onions, chopped
2 large boiled potatoes, peeled	3 tablespoons oil or lard
	7 fresh eggs

Chop the corned beef up with a sharp knife. Do the same with the boiled potatoes, which should be the waxy type.

Fry the chopped onions in oil or lard, using a heavy, shallow skillet; add the chopped meat and potatoes, stirring hard. Then press everything down into the cooking oil with a spatula, and wait a couple of minutes. When an edge of the bottom is seen to be browned, add an egg, and again stir hard; then press down, and wait till the bottom is again browned.

Repeat with the second and third egg.

Now make four nests in the top of the hash and carefully break an egg into each.

Place 4 inches under a broiler and allow the eggs to cook until the yellows begin to lose their sheen.

Total cooking time should be about twenty to twenty-five minutes.

Anglos and Mexicans are most likely to make chile con carne with beef; the Spanish prefer mutton, and call it carne (or *carnero*) con chile. Lamb and mutton are called *carnero* or *cordero,* indiscriminately, in Spanish.

The next two recipes can be switched around, using beef with green chile, or lamb with red. If very young lamb is all that is available—the grades called genuine spring, or even spring—select the shanks, which have the most flavor.

The two unbreakable rules for chile con carne are: (a) never have a greasy film on top and (b) do not use hamburger. No other rule is inflexible when a Southwesterner wants chile, almost anything goes with it.

The first recipe is from Arizona, and the second from New Mexico.

CHILE CON CARNE COLORADO
(*Red Chile with Meat*)

1 cup flour
1 teaspoon oregano
½ teaspoon coriander
    (*cilantro*)
½ teaspoon thyme (*tomillo*)
3 tablespoons fine-ground
    red chile
Pinch cumin (*comino*)

1½ pounds beef in ½-inch
    cubes
1 small onion, minced
2 cloves garlic, mashed and
    minced
2 tablespoons lard
4 cups boiling water

Mix the flour and all the herbs and spices and place in a paper
bag. Toss the meat cubes in the bag until each is thoroughly
coated.

Brown the onions and garlic lightly in lard, and add the floured
meat. When the flour turns golden brown, add 4 cups of boiling
water.

Cook at a light boil until meat is tender.

CARNERA CON CHILE VERDE
(*Lamb or Mutton with Green Chile*)

1½ pounds lamb, in one
    piece
4 cups cold water
12 tiny boiling onions
2 cloves garlic, minced
2 teaspoons oregano

1 teaspoon coriander
    (*cilantro*)
1 four-ounce can green
    chiles
1 ten-ounce can tomatoes

Put the meat in 4 cups of cold water, bring to a boil and skim.
Reduce to a simmer, and cook till meat is tender.

Cube the meat, and remove every trace of fat from the broth.
Warm the broth, if necessary, and put all the ingredients in it;
allow to cook down till liquid is halved.

Hamburger is fine to make a torta, as a meat loaf is called in the Southwest; in Spain the name denotes a cake or pie. In Santa Fe, this dish is usually called *un mitlof*.

TORTA DE CARNE
(*Meat Loaf*)

2 slices stale bread	2 eggs
2 ripe tomatoes, peeled	1 cup Sauce Number Two
1 cup tomato juice	1 tablespoon lard or oil
1½ pounds hamburger, lean	2 cups water

Tear the bread into crumbs, quarter the tomatoes, and mix together thoroughly all ingredients except water and oil.
Heat the lard or oil in a baking pan, form the mixture into a loaf, and place in the pan. Bake at 400° F. until brown all over, then reduce heat to 350°, add 2 cups of water; bake for another hour.

Or bake your favorite meat loaf and pour your favorite hot chile sauce from Chapter 4 over it.
There is an old-time mountain dish whose name I am going to change before I put down the recipe. The original name means Rotted Pot, which would shake off anyone but an experimental turkey buzzard. This sort of humor is more cowboy than Spanish.

LA OLLA SABROSA
(*Savory Pot*)

½ pound boned chicken thighs	Large pinch nutmeg
	Small pinch fennel
½ pound lamb shank, or mutton shoulder, boned weight	Small pinch fine-ground red chile
	1 open piecrust in its tin, pre-baked
½ pound lean pork butt	
½ cup flour	2 ounces dry sherry
Large pinch cinnamon	4 ounces dry red wine
Large pinch allspice	1 tortilla, corn or flour type
Large pinch ground cloves (*clavas*)	

Cube all the meat into bite-size pieces. Put the flour and all the herbs in a paper bag and toss until they are thoroughly mixed; then add the meat, and continue tossing till every cube is thoroughly coated. Put the coated meat in the piecrust, which is still in its tin.

Mix dry sherry and red wine together and moisten a spot on the tortilla with a little of it; moisten the edge with water. Prick the moistened center with a fork. Put the rest of the mixed sherry and wine on the meat, seal top with the tortilla; bake at 350° F. for three hours.

Veal, so far as the northern tier of the Southwest is concerned, can be dismissed quickly; traditionally, there wasn't any. Perhaps because suckling kid, lamb, and pig are so delicious, the mountain farmers try and eat their calves very young, and the result is a watery, tasteless mess.

Down South, however, the Mexican-American brought the

veal cutlet up from Central Mexico, and cooks it in the European manner.

MILANESA
(Veal Cutlet)

2 pounds lean veal, shoulder	Large pinch oregano
or leg cut ¼ inch thick	2 tablespoons parsley,
1 cup flour seasoned with	minced
salt and black pepper	2 eggs
1 cup olive oil	4 cloves garlic
1 cup fresh bread crumbs	

Lay each cut of veal out and pound with the flat edge of a cleaver, or very heavy knife, or with a rubber mallet, till it is twice its size. Sprinkle each piece with the seasoned flour, and set aside for at least twenty minutes.

Start heating the oil in a large skillet.

Mix the bread crumbs, oregano, and parsley and put in a soup dish. Crack the eggs into another soup dish, and stir slightly.

Fry the garlics in the oil till they begin to turn black; remove and discard. Turn the heat down so the oil will not smoke.

Dip each cutlet in the beaten egg and then in the bread crumbs, and fry golden brown.

Wedges of lemon go well with this, and, of course, any Mexican-American home or restaurant has some sort of *salsa picante* available, but I prefer to get my *picante* in a side dish or another course.

Obviously, this dish and its name, widespread through Mexico and the Mexican people of the Southwest, came into the country from Italy; tradition says from an Italian chef who worked for Maximilian and Carlota.

But consider this: when a fried egg is served on top of a *Milanesa*, it becomes a *milanesa holstein*. And Holstein is surely not in Italy, but on the border of Germany and Denmark.

Somebody certainly got around.

Boned, stuffed leg of veal is delicious. In the United States, be sure that the leg is stamped Veal, not Calf; in Mexico or on the border where you can get family-raised calves, this is not so important, as the family sends the children out with the calf to be fattened, and he dines on roadside and streamside greens until he is often as big as his mother while the meat still has the real calf taste.

PIERNA DE TERNERA RELLENA
(*Stuffed Leg of Veal*)

3 strips bacon	1 egg
2 tortillas	2 medium tomatoes, sliced
1 leg veal, about 3 pounds, boned	3 carrots, sliced
1 green chile, seeded to taste	1 large onion, sliced
	2 cups boiling water

Try the bacon out in a heavy skillet; remove the bacon, and fry the tortillas in the fat, adding a little oil if necessary.

Lay the boned leg out flat on a board, inside upward. Pound with a rubber mallet, or the edge of a cleaver, till it is about half as broad as before.

Break up the tortillas and mix them with the chile, chopped, and the bacon, crumbled. Stir in the egg, and mix thoroughly.

Alternate large spoons of this with slices of tomato all down the interior of the leg; roll and tie firmly. Brown the leg in the bacon fat on all sides. Remove and brown the carrot and onion slices in the fat. Put the leg back on this nest of vegetables and add 2 cups of boiling water. Cover and cook in a 300° F. oven, or over low heat on top of the stove till tender, about two hours. Slice crosswise for serving, in thick slices.

The stuffing gets quite heavy and dry, and readily takes up the unthickened sauce.

Pork raising has never been much of a Southwestern industry, but every small landholder used to keep a pig, and most still do.

Here is the old way of dry-curing a ham; the result is a piece of meat that will, without refrigeration, keep for years; the old mountain families never cut into a ham until it had aged for at least a year.

Travelers to Europe tell me that the Spanish do country ham this way, too, but use cayenne instead of chile. It doesn't matter; either way, the initial salt treatment sucks most of the moisture out of the ham and leaves it dry and full of solid flavor; a paper-thin shaving, slowly chewed, would put anyone in a mood of great good humor.

JAMON SECO
(*Dry-cured Ham*)

3 ounces saltpeter	2 ounces black pepper
½ pound brown sugar	¼ pound fine-ground red
2 cups table salt	chile
1 fresh ham	

Mix the saltpeter, sugar, and 1 cup of salt thoroughly, rub it into the ham well. Put in a cool place, and let the salt work on the ham for a full day.

Then rub with the black pepper and the other cup of salt, mixed. Smoke over green scrub oak smoke for ten days. Once a day, throw a handful of cedar (juniper) chips on the oak wood.

When the ham is smoked, rub all over with the chile. Working carefully, so as not to knock the chile off, cover the entire ham in heavy brown paper and seal the paper.

Then make a sling of cheesecloth or muslin, and hang the ham upside down, hock down.

Here is how an uncured ham is cooked in the mountains. The recipe, of course, may be for more than four people if the leg is large; a front leg, called a picnic in the butcher trade, can be used instead of ham.

In the Southwest, the sage is gathered fresh. If you buy dried sage, use a little less.

PIERNO DE MARRANO MONTES
(*Leg of Pork, Mountain-style*)

3 cups Sauce Number Two　　**1 clove garlic, minced**
Large pinch black sage　　**1 small leg of pork**

Simmer the sauce, with the sage and garlic added, until it is a thick paste.

Cut five or six plugs out of the leg and fill them with the paste; replace the meat and secure with toothpicks. About half the paste should be used this way.

Roast at 350° F. half an hour for each pound the leg weighs; half an hour before it is done, spread the rest of the paste over the upper surface of the leg, and raise the temperature to 450° F.

Adobar means to pickle in Spain; it means other methods of cooking in various South American countries. But *carne adovada* (or *adobada*) in Santa Fe always means thin-cut pork chops that have soaked in chile sauce for at least twenty-four hours.

CARNE ADOVADA
(Spiced Pork Chops)

1 tablespoon vinegar	3 tablespoons coarse-ground
1 large yellow onion, in	red chile (*caribe*)
rings	1 teaspoon brown sugar
2 cloves garlic, minced	½ teaspoon oregano
1 tablespoon cooking oil	4 pounds thin-cut end pork
1 teaspoon fine-ground red	chops
chile	

Pour the vinegar over the onion and allow it to stand; brown the garlic in a little oil, add both chiles, stir and thin with water till you have 2 cups. Add the vinegar from the onions, the sugar, and the oregano. Lay the chops on the bottom of a flat dish, put a slice of onion on each, and cover with the sauce. If necessary, repeat in a second layer.
Marinate at least a full day.
Preheat an oven to 250° F., lay the chops out in a baking dish in a single layer without the marinade and sauce, and roast two hours.

When pork chops are breaded (*empanizadas*) they come out very different from the bland *Milanesa* of veal.

COSTILLAS DE PUERCO EMPANIZADAS
(*Breaded Pork Chops*)

2 tablespoons olive oil
2 tablespoons parsley, minced
1 teaspoon dried mint, crumbled
1 clove garlic, minced

1 cup finely grated bread crumbs
4 thick loin pork chops, at least 2 pounds
1 four-ounce can green chiles

Mix the olive oil, parsley, mint, garlic, and bread crumbs into a paste. Pound this in the fleshy part of the chops with the edge of a saucer.

Slowly fry without additional oil or lard until chops are done, turning once.

Remove the chops and keep warm. Seed the canned chiles and cut into long strips; fry in the oil and fat in which the chops cooked. Lay the chile strips on top of chops and serve.

CHAPTER 10

Yardbirds

DOMESTIC POULTRY, MOSTLY CHICKEN AND TURKEY

In Mexican Spanish, poultry are called *aves de corral*, fenced birds or yardbirds. They play a big part in Spanish life in the Southwest, and are badly missed by families who live in our growing cities and are unable to raise a few birds for the table.

Turkey, whether you call it *guajalote, pavo,* or *turqué,* is a party dish, as it is in the Estados Unidos. Turkey *mole* is certainly the royal dish of Mexico, and its use has spread far above the border, through the Southwest and into Colorado and California.

The legend behind this recipe is religious; down south of the border they say that a bishop made an unexpected visit to a convent, and that the sisters were much embarrassed because they had only a simple turkey to serve, and the bishop was French and a noted gourmet.

So they made a sauce of everything available in their kitchen, and *mole* was born. *Mole poblano* is its full name, which seems to translate as Mild Peasant, or Mild Villager, literally.

Perhaps at some time, someplace, they called the turkey a *poblano*. He was the first animal to share village life with the Pueblo Indians, according to archaeological studies.

If you use a whole turkey, the recipe will certainly feed more than four. But turkey legs are often available in the supermarkets, and the dish can be cooked with a small, tough hen. A fryer or roaster would not have enough flavor.

At least one company, La Victoria of Rosemead, California, puts up a canned *mole* powder. It is a little different from the recipe below, as they use three or four kinds of California chile, and Mexican chocolate instead of the Stateside unsweetened. I prefer a simple coarse-ground red chile from the Santa Cruz Valley of Arizona or Velarde or Chimayo, New Mexico, to the blend of chiles *mulatos, pasillas,* and *anchos* the Californians use, but this may be chauvinism.

Certainly, I have never passed up a turkey *mole* in California or Mexico, or any other place it has been available.

If you serve something on the side to take up the sauce, use the broth in a less concentrated form than is recommended below. Refried beans or mashed potatoes go well, if not traditionally, with *mole* sauce.

GUAJALOTE EN MOLE POBLANO
(Turkey in Mole Sauce)

2 turkey legs *or:*
  1 turkey leg and
    second joint
2 quarts water
1 white onion
2 cloves garlic, whole
½ tortilla (corn)
1 French roll
2 tablespoons oil or lard
Pinch coriander *(cilantro)*
Pinch anise *(anis)*

Pinch cumin *(cumino)*
Pinch ground cloves
  (clavas)
½ teaspoon freshly ground
  black pepper
6 tablespoons coarse-ground
  red chile *(caribe)*
2 tablespoons blanched
  almonds
2 squares unsweetened
  chocolate

Put the turkey legs to simmer with the onion and garlic. They should simmer till the meat is ready to slip, not fall, off the bones.

Meanwhile, fry the tortilla and the roll in oil or lard till crisp. Using a mortar or blender, grind the crisp bread up with the herbs, spices, almonds, and chocolate until thoroughly mixed.

Remove the turkey, onion, and garlic from the broth.

Discard the onion and garlic, and cook the broth down to 2 or 3 cups.

Reduce to a simmer, and slowly stir in the blended ingredients. Return the turkey to the sauce, boned or unboned at your preference, and simmer for another twenty minutes.

Green *mole*—*mole poblano* is brown from the chocolate—is much simpler to make than the original dish.

GALLINA EN MOLE VERDE
(Hen in Green Mole Sauce)

1 small fricassee fowl	½ cup chopped parsley
1 four-ounce can green chiles	¼ cup chopped celery leaves
2 tablespoons pumpkin seeds (*pipians*)	Pinch coriander (*cilantro*) Pinch oregano

Barely cover hen with water and simmer until half done. Remove, cut in serving pieces, and return to simmer till done.
Seed the canned chiles, and retain a teaspoonful of the seeds.

Roast these and the pumpkin seeds at 350° F. till they brown. If they start to blacken, remove from oven and toss with a spoon.

Grind all the ingredients, except the fowl, very fine, using a mortar or food mill.

Cook the broth down to ¾ cup and thicken with the ground flavorings; pour over the fowl, and serve.

In Spain, and among the old-timers in northern New Mexico, a dish is called *pepitoria* if it contains both a fowl and the giblets. In Mexico *pepitoria* is a type of candy. In Guatemala, I understand, it is the name for a squash seed.

Here is a delicious New Mexican *pepitoria*, especially good with rice.

PEPITORIA MONTESA
(*Mountain Chicken Stew*)

½ teaspoon saffron	Additional olive oil
½ cup olive oil	1 slice white bread
2 cloves garlic, whole	1 liver (from the hen)
1 stewing hen	1 tablespoon chopped
1 medium white onion,	parsley
chopped	1 large egg yolk,
2 tablespoons piñon kernels,	hard-cooked
roasted or unroasted	½ teaspoon saffron

Use a heavy, covered skillet. As it heats, toast the saffron in it; then add olive oil, and brown the garlic. Remove and discard garlic, and fry the chicken, cut small. As the chicken browns, add the chopped onion; when the onion is soft, cover with water, and reduce heat to simmer; put on skillet lid. In a small skillet, fry the piñons in a little olive oil, stirring steadily until the nuts are golden brown. Break the soft part of the bread up into large crumbs, and fry just as the piñons are finishing. Remove the nuts and bread crumbs to a mortar, and fry the chicken liver in the oil in which they cooked.

Grind the liver, piñons, bread, parsley, egg yolk, and saffron to a paste in the mortar or a blender. Add to the chicken, replace cover, and simmer for an hour. Then remove lid, and allow to simmer for another half hour, or till a leg is tender to a fork.

New Mexicans and the Mexicans of the Southwest do not eat nearly as much rice as do the Spaniards of the old country, but *arroz con pollo,* often called *pollo con arroz* in the English order, has persisted through the years, somewhat changed from the favorite dish of Old Spain.

Mushrooms are added to this pot when available, but are not necessary. The quantity is just about limited to the availability.

ARROZ CON POLLO
(Chicken with Rice)

½ cup cooking, or olive,
   oil
1 cup uncooked rice
1 red onion, chopped
1 frying chicken, 3–4
   pounds

½ teaspoon fine-ground red
   chile
½ teaspoon saffron
12 pitted black olives

Cover the bottom of a heavy skillet with oil, and dump in the uncooked rice. Heat slowly.

Stir vigorously as the rice pops and takes on a peculiar whitish color; when almost all the rice has popped, add the onion and continue stirring. Take out the rice and onion, or push it to a cool side of the skillet, if there is one, and brown the pieces of chicken golden on all sides. Put back the rice and onion and cover the chicken with water. Simmer under a lid till nearly done.

Take out a tablespoonful of the broth and allow it to cool. Dissolve the chile and saffron in the broth and slowly stir them back into the main dish.

Cut the olives in half and stir them in; cook for another five minutes.

For very fine occasions—weddings, perhaps Christmas, the Santa Fe Fiesta—a large roaster or a turkey can be stuffed uniquely and roasted. This is for at least eight people.

GALLINA RELLENA
(Stuffed Fowl)

1 large roaster or small turkey	1 small Hershey bar
	1 cup beef bouillon
¼ pound sweet butter	Large pinch cloves (*clavas*)
½ pound lean hamburger	Large pinch cinnamon
2 tablespoons cooking oil	Large pinch ginger
1 cup currants	Large pinch coriander
4 ounces sherry	(*cilantro*)
4 tablespoons piñon kernels	

Rub the inside and cavity of the fowl with the butter, using up the whole stick.

Brown the hamburger in the oil, breaking it up with a fork as it cooks. Add all else, mix well, stuff the fowl, and roast at 325° F. for about twenty-five minutes per pound.

The next recipe, a modern—and very good—one, calls for boned chicken breasts which self-service markets cannot always supply. The breasts have to be boned raw, or the recipe will fail. The best method is one the Chinese cooks use: use your fingers instead of a knife. Slip your fingertips in between the meat and the bone and slide them along very slowly, feeling your way up to the keel. When one side is loose, do the same on the other, when it will become easy to loose the whole breast from the keel with the tip of a sharp knife.

PECHO DE POLLO ENQUESADO
(*Breast of Chicken in Cheese*)

4 breasts frying chicken	½ cup Parmesan cheese,
1 four-ounce can green	grated
chiles, seeded	½ cup fresh white bread
1 egg	crumbs
Pinch salt	½ pound butter
1 teaspoon olive oil	1 tablespoon lemon juice

Open out the boned breasts and lay a strip of the thoroughly seeded chile inside each. Fold closed, and secure with a toothpick.

Mix the egg, a pinch of salt, and the olive oil in a soup plate. Mix the cheese and the crumbs on a flat plate.

Clarify the butter by melting it over barely simmering water and pouring off the clear upper part; discard the precipate at the bottom. Dip each chicken breast in the egg-oil dish and then in the crumb-cheese dish and chill for at least twenty minutes; several hours is even better.

Heat half the clarified butter quite hot, but not smoking or browning; brown each side of the chicken breasts a light gold; they are done when they yield to a light pressure from your fingertips.

While the chicken is finishing, heat the rest of the clarified butter and the lemon juice together.

Place the chicken on a warm platter and divide the lemon butter over them.

The origin of *pipian* sauce is in dispute. Both the Pueblo Indians and their forebears, the Basket Makers, raised pumpkins and dried seeds; but so did the Indians of the Aztec Empire of Central Mexico. The fact that the New Mexican name for pumpkin is Mexican squash, *calabaza mexicana*, seem to give the nod to southern people.

POLLO EN PIPIAN

(Chicken in Pumpkin Seed Sauce)

½ cup blanched almonds	1 cup popped corn
¾ cup dried pumpkin seeds	1 clove garlic
(*pipians*)	3 cups strong chicken broth
4 cumin seeds (*cominos*)	1 frying chicken, cut up
3 tablespoons coarse-ground	2 tablespoons olive oil
red chile (*caribe*)	Salt

Toss the almonds, pumpkin seeds, and cumin in a hot, dry skillet till they are toasted and the pumpkin seeds turn a shade darker. Grind them in a mortar with the chile, popped corn, and garlic till they are very fine.

Heat a little of the chicken broth, and make a paste of the ground ingredients; keep adding broth until it is all in. Do not salt. Let the sauce simmer down to a good consistency for gravy while the chicken is fried brown on all sides in the olive oil. Pour the sauce over the chicken, and turn heat very low; cook till a fork will pass readily through a chicken leg. Salt to taste at the last moment, as salt will curdle the gravy.

Finally, a recipe for charcoal-grilling chicken. Most barbecue sauces are simply chile sauce, more or less *picante*, usually made with Texas chili powder. This one is obviously Oriental, the invention of one of our great Southwestern Chinese cooks.

If you can't get fresh ginger, use 2 teaspoons of ground ginger and soak it in the wine for half an hour before mixing your marinade. Or omit some of the sugar and use crystallized ginger.

POLLO CHINO
(*Chinese Chicken*)

2½ pounds chicken legs or thighs

2 tablespoons chopped fresh ginger

1 clove garlic, chopped

½ cup white wine

3 green onions, chopped

½ cup soy sauce

1 tablespoon fine-ground red chile

2 tablespoons brown sugar

Marinate the chicken in a mixture of everything else for at least four hours; longer if possible.

Get a good deep bed of charcoal going, and barbecue the chicken about six inches above the heat. Turn frequently, dipping the legs or thighs back into the marinade each time.

Cooking time outdoors depends so much on the temperature, wind, and humidity that it can't be pre-ordained.

Avoid the jackrabbit

COOKING GAME AT HOME AND IN THE FIELD

The Southwest abounds with game, and for each edible animal there is at least one jackrabbit. People—friends of mine and reasonably restrained liars—claim to have cooked jackrabbit to something edible, but I have not been there when they did it.

I mean, I have been hungry and with a rifle or shotgun in my saddle-boot, and it has been near dusk, and I have let jacks hop by me in peace, and gone into camp and eaten meatless beans.

But the cottontail is good, and there is seldom, if ever, a season on him.

Marinating a wild rabbit in water, vinegar, and salt is always advisable; it takes out the gamey taste and softens the meat a little. The length of time doesn't matter.

CONEJO ESTILO VAQUERO
(Rabbit Cowboy-style)

1 rabbit, about 3 pounds, cut up	3 white sage leaves *or:* Large pinch dried sage
2 tablespoons vinegar	Additional salt
2 tablespoons salt	6 slices bacon
1 teaspoon fine-ground red chile	

Soak the cut-up rabbit in cold water to which has been added a couple of tablespoons of vinegar and 2 tablespoons of salt. Remove and dry thoroughly. Rub the chile, sage, and a little salt into a spot on each piece of rabbit.

Cook the bacon slowly in a heavy skillet that can be covered. When the bacon is done, remove, and brown the rabbit on all sides in the bacon fat. Lower the heat—or raise the skillet high above the fire—put the bacon back in on top of the rabbit, cover, and continue cooking about thirty minutes; more if the cottontail is muscular.

The next recipe can also be used for the wild pigeons that migrate through the Southwest. But these pigeons, band-tails, are tough and all simmering time should be raised by half. A mixture of rabbit and pigeons makes a good hunter's stew, *olla cazadora.* It is not necessary to marinate the pigeons in the acidulated, salted water used for the jackrabbit, though some do.

CONEJO DULCE Y AGRIO
(*Sweet-Sour Rabbit*)

1 strip bacon	1 tablespoon brown sugar
4 tablespoons olive oil	2 tablespoons vinegar
1 clove garlic, minced	1 bottle light, preferably
1 medium onion, chopped	Mexican, beer
2 teaspoons fine-ground red	1 ten-ounce can tomatoes
chile	2 tablespoons roasted piñon
1 teaspoon oregano	kernels
1 teaspoon chopped parsley	2 tablespoons seeded raisins
1 rabbit, cut up	

Chop the bacon up small. Put it, the olive oil, garlic, onion, chile, oregano, and parsley in a heavy skillet; heat fairly hot, but not smoking, and brown the rabbit.

Add the brown sugar and vinegar, stir well, and pour in about half the beer. Cover and simmer for a quarter of an hour.

Add the tomatoes, piñons, and raisins; bring to a boil, then reduce to a simmer and cover again.

After another half hour, add the rest of the beer, cover tightly, and bring to a boil.

Uncover at the table for the aroma.

One way to cook pigeons is to marinate them in Sauce Number One for a couple of hours and then roast them till done, about forty-five minutes at 350° F. Ten minutes or so before they are done, lay a slice of bacon over each one.

Mourning doves are plentiful in season, and are not tough, but they are extraordinarily dry. Also, terribly hard to pluck.

The best way to get them ready for cooking is just to skin the breasts out and discard the rest of the bird, still feathered.

Even so, some down will land on the dark little breasts, attracted by some peculiar dove magnetism. Sponge it off with a sponge that has a few drops of vinegar in its water. Then cook them in a manner reminiscent of Old Spain:

PALOMAS A LA MESA DORADA
(Doves on a Golden Mesa)

¼ pound butter	½ teaspoon saffron
¼ cup olive oil	1 cup water
8–12 breasts mourning	1 cup dry white wine
dove	1 cup beef bouillon
1 cup raw rice	½ teaspoon oregano
1 medium white onion,	1 teaspoon parsley, chopped
chopped	

Put half the stick of butter in a heavy skillet that can be covered. Add 2 or 3 tablespoons of oil, and heat quite hot, but not smoking.

Brown the dove meat on all sides, remove, and set aside.

Pop the rice in the oil and butter, but do not brown it; add the onion and stir till it is transparent. Put the doves back in. Dissolve the saffron on top of a cup of water, and add it, the wine, the bouillon, and the herbs. Cover and simmer for half an hour. Dot the breasts with the rest of the butter, cover again, and cook for ten minutes more. Sprinkle with the rest of the olive oil, and serve at once.

Pheasant, widely planted all over the Southwest, is no problem; any chicken recipe can be used. A special one calls for chorizo, the heavily spiced Mexican sausage that may be difficult to obtain away from Mexico or the Southwest. A good substitute precedes the pheasant recipe below.

CHORIZO AL HOGAR
(Home-made Mexican Sausages)

1 pound ground pork	1 teaspoon coriander
1 tablespoon coarse-ground	(*cilantro*)
red chile (*caribe*)	Pinch cumin (*comino*)
1 teaspoon oregano	Pinch ground cloves (*clavas*)

Mix all together thoroughly, and make into four patties. Use in stuffing as is, or try out in a slow skillet until the fat stops running.

FAISAN CON CHORIZOS
(Pheasant with Sausages)

¼ pound bacon	6 ounces port wine
2 plump pheasants	½ teaspoon black pepper
2 medium white onions,	½ teaspoon fine-ground red
chopped	chile
1 pound chorizos	
2 cups cooked prunes, with	
their juice	

Chop the bacon, and brown the pheasants with it.
Add the onions, and fry a minute or two.
In a separate pan, simmer the chorizos or patties in the prune

juice for five minutes. Then drain them, and fry them alongside the pheasants. When they are brown on both sides, lay them on top of the birds.

Add the prunes and prune juice, wine, black pepper, and chile; cover tightly, and cook at 400° F. in an oven, or over medium high heat on top of the stove, for an hour and a half.

I used to know a man who ate venison three hundred days in the year, and would have eaten it more often except that he respected the breeding season. Since he was a United States Forest Service officer, his name is a locked-mouth secret; but in justice to him, I must say that the state he was in had refused the federal government any voice in deer management, and the enforcement of the game laws was not one of his duties.

The following recipe is his:

VENADO BOSQUE
(*Deer of the Woods*)

3 tablespoons fine-ground red chile	12 small turnips
1 quart French dressing	4 ounces currant jelly
1 hind leg of deer	2 large waxy potatoes
3 tablespoons oil or bacon fat	

Mix the chile in the French dressing, and marinate the leg all day, turning it at lunchtime, and basting it from time to time if you can.

Heat the oil or bacon drippings in a roasting pan, and brown the leg on all sides.

Peel and slice the turnips, and put them in the hot fat around the venison. Turn after a moment or two, and divide the jelly amongst them.

Add water to about a half an inch below the turnip tops. If they are small, you will have to add water from time to time as the dish cooks.

Bake at 400° F. for two hours.

Peel and slice thin the potatoes and put them among the turnips and around the leg. Bake for another half hour.

If the deer is very young, especially if it is from a young doe, cut the cooking time accordingly.

The same man used to work ground chile into venison cutlets with the edge of a saucer, fry them in butter, and serve them with applesauce.

Deer ribs are tricky, which works out very well for me, as I gave up hunting when I didn't have to hunt to eat, but still get hungry for the taste of venison. However, my friends share their ribs with me pretty steadily, because of the next recipe, my own invention.

I have used sauerkraut instead of cabbage, in which case I used a rather sweet California white table wine instead of water. Both dishes were good, but I think the fresh cabbage one is a little better.

COSTILLAS DE VENADO
(*Deer Ribs*)

3 tablespoons fine-ground red chile	1 pound butter
1 tablespoon brown sugar	1 head white cabbage
Ribs from one deer	4 medium green apples

Mix the chile and brown sugar; rub the ribs all over with the butter, using up the whole pound, then sprinkle the chile and sugar mixture all over the concave side of the ribs.

Core and shred the cabbage, put it in a roasting pan, cover with water.

Core, peel, and slice the apples.

Lay the ribs, spiced side up, on the cabbage and spread the apple slices over them.

Bake, uncovered, for an hour and a half at 350° F., adding water as needed.

There is only one problem connected with quail, and that is to get enough of them. There is the old story of the man who bet he could eat a quail a day for a month, and after ten days asked if he could substitute a turkey; but I've never been lucky enough to eat quail for ten days running.

CODORNICES SABROSOS
(*Savory Quail*)

8 quails	1 teaspoon oregano
4 tablespoons cooking oil	2 hard-cooked eggs
or bacon fat	1 bottle beer
½ pound liverwurst	
1 teaspoon fine-ground red chile	

Brown the quail in oil or bacon drippings and allow to cool. Mix the liverwurst with the chile, oregano, and grated hard-cooked eggs, using a little of the beer to moisten the mixture if necessary. Stuff the quail with the liverwurst.

Preheat a roasting pan in a 350° F. oven. Put the quail in it,

and add the rest of the beer. Bake, covered, for half an hour; remove cover, reduce heat to 300° F., and bake another fifteen minutes.

If there is too much stuffing, form the remainder into small patties, fry them in butter, and put them in the roasting pan when you remove the cover for the final browning.

※   ※   ※

In the fall the ducks—and a few geese—come up the Colorado and Rio Grande valleys, and the hunters turn out in large numbers. Even a non-hunter gets restless; there is something about the deep Vs in the sky that makes you want to do something—move, travel, get a new job, or just take a shotgun out and pretend you're hunting so your family can eat.

Ducks come fat and lean. Take a sharp knife and make a triangular slit in the breast skin; pull the skin back, and probe the fat. If there is more than the thinnest layer—$\frac{1}{16}$ inch or less—put the duck on a rack in a warm oven—200° F. or so —and try out the fat. Discard it; duck fat is useful for waterproofing boots, and not for much else; and even there, it is advisable not to own a dog, or he will de-waterproof the leather as fast as you grease it.

Having de-fatted your duck, butter him liberally, inside and out, and place a peeled orange, apple, or big white onion in the cavity. Bake at 350° F. and baste with butter; your duck is done when a pricked thigh does not run red.

This is not an exclusive Southwestern recipe, of course. The following one is, but the cook who taught it to me came from Mexico and said he had it from his grandfather, who learned it in Spain. It's a lot of trouble, but worth it.

PATO REAL
(*Royal Duck*)

2 young mallards *or:*	2 large white onions, in
4 ruddy ducks	rings
Giblets from ducks	1 ten-ounce can tomatoes
Pint warm water	1 slice white bread
Pinch marjoram (*mejorano*)	1 four-ounce can green
Pinch thyme (*tomillo*)	chiles, seeded
Pinch rosemary (*romero*)	4 ounces sherry
1 teaspoon black pepper	2 ounces dark rum
Salt	(Mexican, not Jamaican)
1 cup white flour	2 oranges, sliced
4 tablespoons olive oil	12 green ripe olives, pitted
4 cloves garlic	

Place the duck giblets in a pint of warm water, bring to a boil, skim, and reduce to a simmer. Allow them to simmer till they have made a rich broth, and the water is reduced by half.

Mix the herbs with the black pepper, salt, and the flour. Cut the duck up into neat serving pieces, and toss in a paper bag with the flavored flour till they are coated all over.

Heat half the oil in a skillet, and brown 2 cloves of garlic thoroughly; if they burn a little, the flavor will be improved. Remove them and discard. Brown the duck pieces golden in the garlic-flavored oil. Remove them and drain them in a colander in a 200° F. oven.

Render the onion slices transparent in the oil, and then put in the tomatoes. Blend thoroughly with a wooden spoon, add the giblet broth, and put the duck back in. Cover and allow to simmer.

In another skillet, heat the rest of the olive oil; mince the 2 remaining garlics, and fry them gently, not allowing them to do more than brown very faintly. Add the bread, crumbled, and half of one of the chiles, chopped.

Transfer this combination to a mortar and pound it into a paste, moistening with a little of the liquid from the duck pan, if necessary.

Now, remove the duck, and very gently scrape any sauce off the pieces and back into the skillet.

Transfer the sauce from the duck skillet to the mortar or other skillet, and stir contents of both containers together for several minutes while the duck sits in the 200° F. oven.

Pass the sauce back into the first skillet through a strainer or very fine colander. Again, lay the duck in and simmer till nearly done, or when a fork will pass through a thigh, but before there is any tendency for the meat to come off the bones.

Add sherry and rum, and cautiously blend it into the sauce without bruising the nearly done meat.

Raise the oven to 400° F. and bake the unused chiles for five minutes. Turn the oven off and open the door. Place an open flat baking dish, or ovenproof platter, in to warm through.

Put the duck on the platter, pour the sauce over it, and cover the top with a series of chile strips, orange slices, and olives. Place about 4 inches under the grill for three minutes, and serve. Egg noodles or white rice go well with this. Wild rice has too much of its own flavor for the delicate sauce.

CHAPTER 12

Homegrown

DRIED AND FRESH VEGETABLES

In the northern Southwest, or Upper Sonoran life zone, the growing season is short; the tomato will not, in the open, mature, though a few gardeners are now using new varieties with some success.

But, traditionally, the tomato came up from the southern part of the territory, in trade, and was then sun-dried to a paste that could flavor things all winter. Those tomatoes from the New Mexico-Texas border have a wonderful flavor, and we use them—canned at Anthony, New Mexico-Texas—in preference to the finest of fresh tomatoes from the Lower Rio Grande or California. As a straight vegetable, open a ⚹300 or ⚹303 can, sprinkle with a little oregano, a little thyme, and a teaspoonful of chile and either heat or allow to stand in the refrigerator for a couple of hours.

The anthropologists refer to the Pueblo Indian culture as

one of squash-bean-corn; the tradition has not been broken by us later immigrants to the area, the Navajo-Apache, Spanish, and Anglo.

Everything was dried in the hot Southwestern sun, except onions and garlic, which were braided and hung in the shade, either in the kitchen itself, or in brush shelters, called *ramadas*. The green chiles were braided and hung against the adobe walls to turn red in long *ristras*. Were, nothing; they still are, and make the countryside through such towns as Truchas and Trampas, Chimayo and Velarde, Taos and Dixon a delight in the early fall.

Pumpkins and other large squash were quartered and stuck up on sticks, where the barnyard animals couldn't get them. Smaller squash, small fruits, fava and lima beans, bolitos and other *frijoles* were laid in trays on the roof, when possible covered with cheesecloth, and sunbaked; so were orchard fruits,

but they were broken open and stoned or sliced first, except for plums, which dried whole.

Grapes were tied in bunches to hoops or sticks laid from tree to tree or tree to roof, and when dried into raisins, were taken to the storeroom still fastened to the wood.

But, before the chiles dried red, everyone ate *chiles rellenos.* Today, with canned chile, we can eat it all year round, which is why we do not refer to the old days as good.

The traditional *chiles rellenos* were made with fresh green chiles, roasted in the oven, steamed in a hot wet cloth and then peeled. We use canned chiles. The old-time Spanish liked the almost tasteless Monterey Jack cheese; we use the sharpest Cheddar we can find.

Some pour a hot chile sauce—any of those from Chapter 4 —over their *chiles rellenos.* This, to me, is like dropping perfume on a carnation.

Two *chiles rellenos* on either side of a thin strip of steak or a single trout, are all the main course any dinner needs. Three *chiles rellenos* are a pretty darned good meal, too.

CHILES RELLENOS
(*Stuffed Chiles*)

1 tablespoon flour	3 tablespoons cooking oil
4 fresh eggs	or lard
8 canned green chiles	
1 pound Cheddar, sliced thick	

Whip the flour up in the eggs to make a thin batter; a little water may be added if desired.

Take as many seeds out of the chiles as is needed to reduce the heat (*picante*). Lay the cheese inside the chiles evenly. Drag each chile through the egg batter, first one side up, then the other. Drain any surplus batter back into the dish and repeat till most of the batter is used up.

Heat the oil or lard very hot and lay the chiles in it.

Turn after five minutes, pour any leftover batter over the chiles, and fry for another five minutes. If any egg is left uncooked, tip the skillet; the batter will run down and catch in the fried batter and cheese sticking out of the chiles.

When freshly shelled corn is sun-dried, it becomes chicos, which have a different taste than fresh, canned, or frozen corn. It is almost as though some of the lazy, spicy flavor of heavy sunlight had gone into them. If you can't get chicos, frozen kernel corn is second best.

FRIJOLES CON CHICOS
(*Beans and Corn*)

½ cup chicos
1 cup pinto beans or 1 cup pink beans
¼ pound salt pork

Soak the chicos and beans overnight in cold water.
Dice the salt pork in ¼-inch cubes, and try out over gentle heat in a heavy skillet.
Combine the chicos and beans in a heavy pot and just cover with cold water, preferably rain or spring water.
Scrape the salt pork and fat into the pot, and stir 3 times.
Bring to just below a boil and reduce at once to a simmer. Simmer for four to six hours, depending on the altitude and how long the beans have been stored.

A similar dish can be made with dried limas or favas (habas, horsebeans), in which case a few cut-up pimentos or a red bell pepper adds flavor.

People with a limited supply of meat, like the Chinese and the old New Mexico-Arizona mountain people, fry their vegetables to give them a meaty taste.

CALABACITAS
(*Summer Squash*)

1 pound summer squash, diced	1 four-ounce can green chiles, chopped
1 small yellow onion	2 ounces milk
2 tablespoons lard or bacon drippings	¼ pound grated cheese

Fry the squash and onion in the lard over medium heat till they take up the fat.

Add the chiles, stir, and slowly pour in the milk.

Reduce the heat so the milk does not curdle.

Simmer for fifteen minutes, add the cheese, stir once and serve.

Quelites, lamb's quarters (white goosefoot, pigweed, *Chenopodium*), are also fried after boiling, with the addition of a little green chile and a small onion. I've tried them, and to me they need doctoring with butter and soy sauce.

The truth is, vegetables are not a great Southwestern specialty. People who eat chile daily do not need vitamins; both the red and the green form furnish just about all the alphabet of diet supplements, a number of trace minerals, and a general feeling of euphoria; what more do you need?

If you can get hold of some very large white onions—the kind called Bermudas in many markets—here is a very good, mildly enchilied dish:

CEBOLLAS RELLENAS
(*Stuffed Onions*)

4 Bermuda onions	2 tablespoons butter
Salt	½ teaspoon oregano
½ cup chopped leftover	½ teaspoon parsley, chopped
meat	1 cup bread crumbs
½ cup canned chopped	1 cup milk
green chiles	½ cup water

Peel the onions, and cut a thin slice off each end.

Stab the center of each onion from the top in several places, being sure not to pierce the outside layer.

Drop into boiling water (salted) and cook till nearly tender.

Cool and carefully scoop out the inside.

Chop the scraped-out onion up with the meat, chiles, butter, herbs, and about three-quarters of the bread crumbs. Stuff the onions, allowing the mixture to dome up as needed.

Sprinkle the remaining bread crumbs over the domes, place the onions in a baking pan, with the milk and half a cup of water. Bake half an hour at 375° F.

Any kind of thin-skinned squash can be used in the next recipe; or thick-skinned squash, such as the acorn, can be parboiled and the pulp used.

The old-timers, of course, ate this dish a good deal in winter, pre-soaking the sun-dried squash.

Don't bother to dry your squash, as the process doesn't add a thing to the *calabacita;* but dried apples are better in this dish than fresh ones.

CALABACITAS AGRIAS Y DULCES
(Sweet and Sour Squash)

1 pound summer squash	2 tablespoons vinegar
¼ pound dried apples,	1 tablespoon brown sugar
soaked	½ tablespoon sweet basil
2 tablespoons oil or butter	(*albahaca*)

Cut the squash into fairly thick slices. Fry the squash and the rehydrated apples, drained, in the oil or butter for a few minutes (lard will not do).

Scoop out the squash and apples with a slotted spoon, allow the oil or butter to drain back into the skillet. Place the fruit and vegetable in a baking dish.

Add the vinegar and sugar to the skillet, and cook, stirring constantly for two minutes. Pour the contents of the skillet over the contents of the baking dish, sprinkle with the sweet basil and bake ten minutes at 300° F.

This can be eaten hot or cold.

CHAPTER 13

The sweet land!

SOUTHWESTERN AND MEXICAN DESSERTS

Down near Nogales, I was having the evening meal—simply called *comida*, or meal, in that house—with a very aged gentleman who had crossed from Mexico at El Paso in 1921.

When his granddaughter announced sadly that, since she had not expected us back so soon, there was no sweet with which to end the meal, he cried: "The land is so sweet, we need no other."

But Mexicans, Spanish, and Anglos alike are fond of desserts. Mexicans can, apparently, eat flan, which is caramel custard, two or three times a day, and I have never had a bad flan served to me anyplace in the southern Southwest or in Mexico.

FLAN
(Custard, the National Dessert of Mexico)

1 cup brown sugar	2 large cans evaporated
2 egg whites	milk
2 teaspoons vanilla	6 tablespoons Mexican rum,
4 egg yolks	light or dark
¾ cup white sugar	

Divide the brown sugar among four custard cups.

Place cups in a saucepan, filled halfway up the cups with water, and bring to a boil.

When the sugar melts and turns golden, take tongs or a pot holder, and tilt each cup around until the caramelized sugar coats the wall of the cup halfway up. At once take the cups out of the boiling water and allow them to cool quickly.

While they are doing so, beat the egg whites, vanilla, egg yolks, and white sugar with a French whisk or a rotary eggbeater, gradually adding the canned milk.

When the sugar is dissolved, pour into the four custard cups. Put them in a baking pan containing about an inch of water, cover each cup—a demitasse saucer does fine—and bake at 350° F. for an hour. Turn Flan out onto their serving plates, pour rum over them, and light for the table.

In the northern Southwest, I have eaten a very passable dessert made by pouring 2 cans of condensed (not evaporated or canned cow) milk into a pumpkin, which was then baked and quartered. Tilt it once in a while during baking so that the sweet milk clings to all the pumpkin's shreds.

I've heard this simple dish called *calabaza al horno,* or pumpkin in the oven; it is also sometimes called *dulce bruto,* or country sweet, which I like better.

Natilla is a variant on flan, and more likely to be found in our northern counties than in the south.

NATILLAS
(*Boiled Custard*)

4 eggs	3 tablespoons white flour
4 cups milk	Cinnamon
¾ cup white sugar	

Separate the eggs, and beat the whites until dry. Heat the milk to just below boiling, and pour the whipped egg whites onto the top, carefully and slowly. Watch closely so that the milk does not boil. In about five minutes the whites will have cooked to a sort of meringue; the top of the floating island will feel dry and warm to the touch.

Scoop out the cooked whites and put in a mixing bowl. Turn off the heat under the milk, and beat the milk with the egg yolks, sugar, and flour; turn the heat on again, very low, and cook until the mixture thickens.

Pour into the whites, and sprinkle the cinnamon on top. Serve hot or cold.

A *capirote,* in classical Spanish, is a sort of cape or hood worn over the head by various religious, college students, or masqueraders in a parade. How the name came to be attached to a New Mexican bread pudding, time only knows; someone must have had better imagination than he did eyesight.

Fresh lard must be used in making *capirotadas;* oil or butter will not do.

CAPIROTADAS
(Bread Pudding)

½ cup piñon nuts, salted	¼ cup powdered sugar
½ cup seedless raisins	Leaf lard for deep frying
4 slices fresh white bread	1 teaspoon cinnamon
1 egg	

Poke the piñons and raisins all over the slices of bread and brown lightly in the oven.

Separate the egg, and beat the white dry; then add the yolk and a little sugar and beat again.

Dip the bread in the egg mixture and fry in deep lard until golden.

Sprinkle each slice of bread with the rest of the sugar and cinnamon, mixed.

There is also a *capirotada* that contains onion, tomato, and cheese along with the sugar and egg, and raisins. The recipe will not be passed along.

However, I've eaten a southern Arizona *capirotada* that had fresh Monterey Jack cheese in it. It was very good, but to my taste is even better if Philadelphia cream cheese is used.

CAPIROTADA DEL SUR
(*Southern Bread Pudding*)

½ pound brown sugar
Pint warm water
6 cloves
1 stick cinnamon
2 pieces crystallized ginger
3 cups croutons
¼ pound cream cheese or
fresh Monterey Jack
cheese

¼ cup piñons
½ cup raisins
¼ cup crushed peanuts
2 medium apples, sliced

Dissolve the sugar in a pint of warm water; put in a double boiler, and add the cloves, cinnamon, and crystallized ginger. Keep over simmering water till needed.

Butter a casserole, and cover the bottom with croutons. Cube the cream cheese, and put a thin layer over the croutons; sprinkle with piñons, raisins, and crushed peanuts.

Cover with a layer of apple slices. Repeat as possible, ending with apple slices. Strain the flavored sugar water over the pudding, and bake at 350° F. for thirty minutes.

Both north and south, there is a trick with junket that is very different from the way it is treated in the rest of the United States. The name for this dish puzzled me for a while, as *chango* means monkey both in Mexican and New Mexican. Then I saw it spelled out; the name is colloquial for a tuft of hair.

CHONGITOS
(*Little Tufts*)

2 egg yolks	2 cups sugar
1 quart milk	½ teaspoon cinnamon,
3 junket tablets	ground
2 cups water	1 teaspoon vanilla

Beat the egg yolks and the milk together.

Dissolve the tablets in a little warm water, and stir into the milky mixture. Leave the mixture in a warm place till it dissolves. Cool thoroughly.

Heat 2 cups of water to boiling, and dissolve the sugar in it; stir in the cinnamon and vanilla.

Drop tablespoons of the junket into the boiling syrup, reduce the heat, and allow to simmer for thirty minutes.

Remove the *Chongitos* and chill them; cook the syrup down to the consistency of good maple syrup and pour, hot, over the little knots and serve.

CHIMICHANGOS DULCES DE TUBAC
(*Sweet Thingumabobs from Tubac*)

4 cups sifted white flour,	Water
all purpose	Flour for dusting, butter for
1½ teaspoons salt	greasing hands
½ teaspoon cinnamon	Lard for deep frying
½ cup lard	

Mix the three dry ingredients thoroughly; cut in the lard with a knife; add enough water to make the dough slightly elastic—the amount of water seems to vary with the climate.

Cut the dough into lumps about the size of an egg, and chill for half an hour.

Powder a bread board and massage your hands thoroughly with

butter. Put a lump of dough on the board and pat it till it is as big in diameter as the largest skillet you own or can borrow. Put the skillet over a moderate heat, and warm it till a drop of water dances and steams away.

Lay each tortilla in the skillet for a minute on each side; remove and stack tortillas and set them aside.

FILLING:

¼ **cup granulated sugar**	¼ **cup unsalted butter**
½ **teaspoon grated lemon**	**Lard for deep frying**
rind	**Powdered sugar for dusting**
2 **cups stewed fruit, such**	
as apricots or dried apples	

Stir the sugar and lemon rind into the stewed fruit; bring to a boil and allow to cool.

Fold each tortilla 2 inches down from the top and up from the bottom; spread the fruit mixture from fold to fold about 2 inches wide and 2 inches in from the right-hand edge; spread the butter for about an inch just in from the fruit mixture.

Roll the tortilla from right to left around the fruit.

Heat the lard to 370° F. and drop the chimichangos in one by one; remove the same way as they turn the color of golden toast. Drain on brown paper, sprinkle with powdered sugar, and serve hot.

The beaver-tail cactus grows from coast to coast in the southern part of the United States—I have found them on a rocky outcropping in the middle of Birmingham, Alabama, for instance—but so far as I know, only Arizonans make candy out of the fruit.

This is the prickly pear, and before trying to peel it, be

sure to scorch the prickles off. Then peel the fruit, seed it, weigh it, and cook it up with an equal weight of sugar. Simmer slowly till the fruit is dissolved, strain through cheesecloth and allow the candy to jell. Cut it in squares and toss it with powdered sugar, and you have an irresistible sweet.

In the northern valleys, a similar candy is made from quinces; the method is identical, and quince candy has a sweet-sour taste that is unusual.

Incidentally, the prickly pear is called *tuna* in Spanish, and the tuna fish is called *atún*, to relieve the puzzlement of travelers who find canyons or towns or mesas called La Tuna miles from salt water.

Empanadas filled with meat are very similar to Cornish pasties; filled with a sweet mixture, such as applesauce flavored with cinnamon, any kind of jelly or jam, or flan, they are a favorite sweet, used for dessert to restoke kids when they come home from school.

EMPANADITAS
(*Pastry Cases*)

2 cups white flour	⅓ cup leaf lard
3 teaspoons baking powder	Powdered sugar
2 tablespoons sugar	Lard for deep frying
Pinch salt	

Sift the dry ingredients into a bowl, and cut in the lard with a knife or saucer edge. Use your hands as little as possible. Add ice water till dough holds together. Lift out with a chilled cooking spoon, and lay on a floured board. Roll out till very thin, and cut into circles 3 inches in diameter.

Lay a generous spoonful of filling on one round, moisten the edge of the dough with cold water, and press another circle of dough on top, as in ravioli.

Lift with a spatula and drop into hot, deep fat; when *Empanadita* turns golden brown, it is done; drain on brown paper, and sprinkle with powdered sugar.

The walnut trees—nogales—that give their name to so many points in the Southwest, have pretty much disappeared. They were native black walnuts, hard as the devil to shell, but worthwhile. If you can't get black walnut meats in the market—try a confectioner's—English walnuts will do.

PUDIN DE NOGALES
(*Walnut Pudding*)

½ pound walnut meats	1 cup white sugar
1 teaspoon ground cinnamon	2 tablespoons unsalted butter
5 eggs	

Pound the nut meats in a mortar with the cinnamon until you have a smooth paste every bit of which tastes of cinnamon.

Beat the eggs with a wire whisk, gradually adding the sugar and then the flavored paste.

Butter a mold, and set it in a pan filled with enough water to come well up the side of the mold, but not to splash into the pudding if the water inadvertently boils. It shouldn't; keep it at a simmer till a straw comes out clean.

At once turn the pudding out, and let it stand till cold.

Every old-time family had a heavy iron mold in the shape of a lamb; this was only brought out at Easter, and filled with egg pudding. Nowadays, lamb-shaped molds are made of aluminum, but they will do; so will any mold with a cover.

PUDIN PASCUAL
(*Easter Pudding*)

2 cups brown sugar	2 ounces fresh pork fat,
1 teaspoon grated lemon	unsalted and in one piece
rind	12 egg yolks
½ teaspoon ground cinnamon	½ cup port wine
½ teaspoon dried, powdered	
mint	

Melt the sugar and add the lemon rind, cinnamon, mint, and the pork fat. Place over boiling water and whip until it homogenizes, and the flavor is the same at any point.

Use as much of this syrup as is necessary to coat, very thinly, the lining of a covered mold.

While you are doing this, let your syrup cool a little. Then beat in the eggs and the wine, thoroughly, and pour into the mold. Cover and place in a pan of boiling water.

Reduce the heat to a simmer, and cook for an hour.

Finally, a little something that the old-timers, with their passion for mint, used to nibble with the after-dinner coffee. Of course, they had never heard of dining rooms; they ate in the kitchen, and while the men argued heavily, the lady of the house would make these tidbits and bring them to the table hot. Then she'd go back and make some more, endlessly.

DULCES DE YERBABUENA
(*Mint Tidbits*)

1 bunch big mint stalks	1 pint milk
1½ cups fresh lard	2 tablespoons sweet butter
1 cup flour	½ cup powdered sugar
1 egg	

Wash the mint thoroughly, and dry it with a towel. Pick it over, rejecting small stalks or brown ones.

Heat the lard very hot, but not smoking.

While it is heating, make a batter of the flour, egg, milk, and the butter, melted.

Dip the stalks in the batter one at a time, drop into the hot lard, take out after a minute and drain on brown paper.

Sprinkle with the powdered sugar, and eat at once.

But don't just taste the Southwest; come visit us.

Santa Fe, New Mexico
Tubac, Arizona

INDEX

Aguacate y Pamplemusa, 34
Albondigas Mexicanas, 23–24
Angel's Blood Cocktail, 5
Appetizers and Cocktails, 1–9
  Angel's Blood, 5
  Avocado Dip, 2
  Bean Dip, 3–4
  Chile and Cheese Dip, 2–3
  Crisp Small Tortillas, 9
  Fish Cocktail, 7–8
  Guacamole, 2
  Margarita Cocktail, 4–5
  Seafood Cocktails, 6–8
  Shrimp Cocktail, 8
Arroz con Pescado, 80–81
Arroz con Pollo, 130–31
Asadito, 103–4
Avocado Dip, 2
Avocado and Grapefruit, 34

Bacalao Fronterizo, 70–71
Bacalao Nuevo Mexico, 70
Backbone of Mexico (Beans), 50–51
Barbecuing, 104–6
Barbo Verde, 74–75
Bass with Rice, 80–81
Beans, 45–58 (*See also* Chick-peas)
  Backbone of Mexico, 50–51
  Bolitas, 47–50
  Burritos with, 86
  with Cheese, Refried, 53
  in Chile Sauce, 3–4
  and Corn, 153

of Dawn, 54
Dip of, 3–4
Drunken Horse, 55
Horse, 54
  Drunken, 55
  Mexican Delight, 52
  with Milk, 49–50
  Mountain, 52
  New Orleans Red, 51
  Palomar-style, 46–47
  Salad of Green, 30
  Savory, 53
Beef, 107, 110–12
  Chile con Carne, 115
  Hash, Corned, 113–14
  Meatball Soup, 22–23
  Meatballs with, 23–24
  Meat Loaf, 116
  Prime Ribs, 110
  Short Ribs, Cowboy, 105
  Soup
    Dawn Broth, 12
    Meatball, 22–23
  Steak,
    Nogales-style, 112
    Santa Fe, 111
  Tacos, 90
Beet Salad, Chilled, 27–28
Betabel Friolento, 27–28
Blood Pudding, Kid's, 102
Blue Trout, 73
Bolitas, 47–48
Bolitas con Leche, 49–50

Border Style Salt Cod, 70–71
Borrego, 100ff.
Borrego al Horno, 101
Bread Pudding, 160
  Southern, 161
Burritos, 86–87

Cabezita, 102–3
Cabrito, 100ff.
Cabrito Asado, 100–1
Cactus (*Nopales*), 76–77
  Fish and, 78
Calabacitas, 153–54
Calabacitas Agrias y Dulces, 155
Calabaza al Horno, 158
Caldo de Albor, 12
Caldo con Bolitas de Leche, 21–22
Caldo Colado, 13
Camarones de Nogales, 68–69
Capirotada del Sur, 161
Capirotadas, 160
Carne Adovada, 122
Carne Estilo Nogales, 112
Carnera con Chile Verde, 115
Carne Santa Fe, 111
Catfish, 74
  Green, 74–75
Cauliflower, Cold, 32–33
Cebollas Rellenas, 154–55
Cecis. See *Garbanzos*
Ceviche de Camarones, 8
Ceviche de Pescado, 7–8
Cheese (See also *Enchiladas; Tacos*)
  Breast of Chicken in, 133
  and Chile Dip, 2–3
  Chiles Stuffed with, 151–52
  Refried Beans with, 53
Chicken
  in Cheese, Breast of, 132–33
  Chinese, Charcoal-grilled, 134–35
  Enchiladas, 92–93
  in Green Mole Sauce, 128–29
  in Pumpkin Seed Sauce, 134
  with Rice, 130–31
  Savory Pot with, 117
  Stew, Mountain, 130

Stuffed Roast, 132
Tacos, 88–90
Chick-peas (*Garbanzos*), 18, 55
  Baked, 56–57
  in Green Chile Sauce, 56
  Shepherd's, 57–58
  Soup of, 19
  Soused (Salad), 35
Chile con Carne, 114–15
  Green, 115
  Red, 115
Chile con Carne Colorado, 115
Chile and Cheese Dip, 2–3
Chile Enchiladas, Red, 93–94
Chilepequins, 47
Chile con Queso, 2–3
Chiles, xii–xiii
  Chilepequins, 47
  Drying of, 150
  Jalapeños, 50
  Stuffed, 151–52
Chile Salad, Green, 27
Chile Sauce (*See also* specific dishes
    using Chile Sauce)
  Coarse-ground Red (Number 2),
    38–39
  Dark Red (Number 4), 40
  Fresh (Number 7), 42–43
  Hot (Number 1), 38
  Hot, Green (Number 6), 42
  Santa Fe (Number 5), 41
  Spanish Omelet, 65–66
  Two (Number 3), 39–40
Chiles Rellenos, 151–52
Chimichangos, 87
Chimichangos Dulces de Tubac,
    162–63
Chinese Chicken, 135
Chongitos, 162
Chorizo al Hogar, 141
Chorizo Sausage, 17–18
  Chick-peas in Green Chile Sauce
    with, 56
  Home-made, 141
  Pheasant with, 141–42
  Unsplit Pea Soup with, 18

Chuletas de Carnero con Piñones, 110
Chuletas de Carnero Sabrosas, 109
Clear Broth, 13
Cocktails, 4–5
  Angel's Blood, 5
  Margarita, 4–5
Cocktails, Seafood, 6–8
  Fish, 7–8
  Shrimp, 8
Coctel Margarita, 4–5
Cod
  Border-style Salt, 70–71
  with Greens, Salt, 71–72
  New Mexican Salt, 70
Codornices Sabrosos, 145
Coliflor Fria, 32–33
Conejo Dulce y Agrio, 139
Conejo Estilo Vaquero, 138
Corn, 83–98
  Dried (*Chicos*), 152
    Beans and, 153
  Husks, 95–96
  Enchiladas, 87, 92–95
  Masa (Mexican Dough), 84
  Tacos, 87–92
  Tamales, 95–98
  Tortillas (See *Tortillas*)
  Tostados, 87
Costillas Falsas Estilo Vaquero, 105
Costillas de Puerco, 106
Costillas de Puerco Empanizadas, 123
Costillas de Venado, 143–44
Country Green Sauce, 43–44
Cowboy Short Ribs, 105
Custard
  Balls, Broth with, 21
  Boiled, 159
  Flan, 157–58

Dark Red Sauce, 40
Dawn Broth, 12
Deer Ribs, 143–44
Deer of the Woods, 142–43
Desserts, 157–67
  Boiled Custard, 159

Bread Pudding, 160
  Southern, 161
  Easter Pudding, 165–66
  Flan, 157–58
  Little Tufts, 162
  Mint Tidbits, 166–67
  Pastry Cases, 164–65
  Prickly Pear Candy, 163–64
  Pumpkin, 158
  Sweet Thingumabobs from Tubac, 162–63
  Walnut Pudding, 165
Dips
  Avocado, 2
  Bean, 3–4
  Cheese and Chile, 2–3
Doves, 139–40
  on a Golden Mesa, 140
Drunken Horse Beans, 55
Duck, 146–48
  Royal, 147–48
Dulces de Yerbabuena, 166–67

Easter Pudding, 165–66
Egg Fritters, 62–63
Eggplant, Tacos with, 91–92
Eggs, 59–66
  Beans of Dawn with, 54
  Corned Beef Hash with, 113–14
  Fritters, 62–63
  in the Nest, 63–64
  Rancher's, 59–61
    Border, 60–61
    Northern, 60
    Spanish, 61
  Red Chile Enchiladas with, 93–94
  Spanish Omelet Sauce, 65–66
  Sweet and Hot, 62
  Tortilla with, 66
Empanaditas, 164–65
Enchiladas, 87, 92–95
  Chicken, 92–93
  Green, 95
  Red Chile, 93–94
Enchiladas Coloradas, 93–94
Enchiladas de Pollo, 92–93
Enchiladas Verdes, 95

Ensalada de Chiles Verdes, 27
Ensalada de Ejotes, 30
Ensalada de Papas, 29–30
Ensalada de Pastor, 26
Ensalada de Pimientos Dulces, 31
Ensalada de Primavera, 34–35
Ensalada de Quelites, 28–29

Faisan con Chorizos, 141–42
Favas Borrachas, 55
Fish (and Shellfish), 67–81
  and Cactus, 78
  Catfish, Green, 74–75
  Cocktails, 6–8
  Cod, Salt, 70–72
    Border-style, 70–71
    with Greens, 71–72
    New Mexican, 70
  Indian Roe, 69
  Perch, Fresh, 75
  with Potatoes, 78–79
  with Rice, 80–81
  Shrimp Fritters, 68
  Shrimps from Nogales, 68–69
  Sunfish, 76
  Trout, 67, 72–74
    Blue, 73
    Fried Mountain, 72–73
    Stuffed, 73–74
Flan, 157–58
Flour Tortillas, 85–86
  Burritos, 86–87
  Chimichangos, 87
  Chimichangos Dulces de Tubac, 162–63
French influence, xi. *See also* specific dishes
Frijoles de Albor, 54
Frijoles con Chicos, 153
Frijoles Criollos, 51
Frijoles Estilo Palomar, 46–47
Frijoles Mexicanos, 50–51
Frijoles Montes, 52
Frijoles Refritos, 52
Frijoles Sabrosos, 53

Fritters
  Egg, 62–63
  Shrimp, 68

Gallina en Mole Verde, 128–29
Gallina Rellena, 132
Game, 137–48
  Deer Ribs, 143–44
  Deer of the Woods, 142–43
  Doves, 139–40
    on a Golden Mesa, 140
  Duck, 146–48
    Royal, 147–48
  Pheasant with Sausages, 141–42
  Pigeons, Roast, 139
  Pigeons, Sweet Sour, 138–39
  Quail, Savory, 145–46
  Rabbit, 137–39
    Cowboy-style, 138
    Sweet-Sour, 139
  Venison, 142–44
Garbanzos (Chick-peas), 18, 55
  Baked, 56–57
  in Green Chile Sauce, 56
  Shepherd's, 57–58
  Soup of, 19
  Soused (Salad), 35
Garbanzos en Chile Verde, 56
Garbanzos Encurtidos, 35
Garbanzos al Horno, 56–57
Garbanzos de Pastor, 57–58
German influence, xii. *See also* specific dishes
Grapefruit and Avocado, 34
Grapes, Drying of, 151
Guacamole, 2
Guajalote en Mole Poblano, 127
Guide to the Fishes of New Mexico, 74

Ham
  Drunken Horse Beans with, 55
  Dry-cured, 120–21
Harvey, Fred, xii
Hominy, Tripe Soup with, 20–21
Hot Sauce, 38
  Green, 42

Huevas Indias, 69
Huevos Dulces y Picantes, 62
Huevos al Nido, 63–64
Huevos Rancheros, 59–61
Huevos Rancheros Estilo Gachupin,
  61
Huevos Rancheros de la Frontera,
  60–61

Indian Roe, 69

Jalapeños, 50
Jamon Seco, 120–21
Junket, Little Tufts, 162

Kid, 100
  Blood Pudding, 102
  Little Head, 102–3
  Little Roast (Ribs), 103–4
  Roast, 100–1
Koster, William J., 74

Lamb, 100, 107, 108–10
  Breast, Riblets of, 104
  Broth with Custard Balls, 21–22
  Chile con Carne with, 114–15
  Chops, Savory, 109
  Chops with Piñon Nuts, 110
  Leg of, 108–9
  Little Head, 102–3
  Little Roast (Ribs), 103–4
  in the Oven, 101
  Savory Pot with, 117
  Shepherd's Chick-peas with, 57–58
Lamb's Quarters, 71
  Fried, 154
  Salt Cod with, 71–72
Little Head, 102–3
Little Roast, 103–4
Little Tufts, 162

Margarita Cocktail, 4–5
Masa, 84
Masa Harina, 84
Meat, 99–123 (*See also* Game;
  Poultry; specific meats)
  Savory Pot, 117

Spanish Hash, 113
Stuffed Onions, 154–55
Tamale Pie, 97–98
Tamales, 97
Meatballs, Mexican, 23–24
Meatball Soup, 22–23
Meat Loaf, 116
Menudo Nuevo Mexicano, 20
Menudo con Posole, 20–21
Mescal, 4
Mexican Delight (Beans), 52
Mexican Dough, 84
Mexican Influence, xi. *See also* spe-
  cific dishes
Mexican Meatballs, 23–24
Mexican Sausages. *See* Chorizo
  Sausage
Milanesa, 118–19
Mint Tidbits, 166–67
Mole Poblano, 125–27
Mole Sauce, 125–26
  Chicken in Green, 128–29
  Turkey in, 127
Morcilla de Cabrito, 102
Mountain Beans, 52
Mountain Chicken Stew, 130
Mountain Trout, Fried, 72–73
Mourning Doves, 139–40
  on a Golden Mesa, 140
Mutton
  Boiled Dish, 107–8
  Chile con Carne with, 114–15

Natillas, 159
New Mexican Salt Cod, 70
New Orleans Red Beans, 51
Nido, Sara, 5
Nogales-style Steak, 112
Nopales, 76–77
  Fish with, 78

Olives, 1
Olla Sabrosa, La, 117
Omelet Sauce, Spanish, 65–66
Onions,
  Green, 14
  Stuffed, 154–55

Palomar-style Beans, 46–47
Palomas a la Mesa Dorada, 140
Pastry Cases, 164–65
Pato Real, 147–48
Pea Soup, Unsplit, 18
Pecho de Pollo Enquesado, 130
Peopitoria Montesa, 130
Peppers (*See also* Chiles)
  Bell, 30–31
Pepper Salad, Sweet, 31
Perca Fresca, 75
Perch, Fresh, 75
Pescado con Papas, 78–79
Pescados con Nopales, 78
Pheasant with Sausages, 141–42
Picadillo, 113
Picadillo de Carne Salmuerado, 113–14
Pie, Tamale, 97–98
Pierna de Carnero, 108–9
Pierna de Ternera Rellena, 119–20
Pierno de Marrano Montes, 121
Pigeon
  Roast, 139
  Sweet-Sour, 138–39
Piñon Nuts, 22
  Lamb Chops with, 110
Pipian Sauce, 133–34
Pollo Chino, 135
Pollo en Pipian, 134
Pork, 121–23
  Barbecued Spareribs, 106
  Chops, Breaded, 123
  Chops, Spiced, 122
  Leg of, Mountain-style, 121
  Meatballs with, 23–24
  Soup, Clear Broth, 13
  Sausage. *See* Chorizo Sausage
  Savory Beans with, 53
  Savory Pot with, 117
  Tacos with Marinated, 90–91
  Tamales, 96
Potato Salad, 29–30
  Fish with, 78–79
Poultry, 125–35. *See also* Chicken;
  Turkey

Prickly Pear, 76
  Candy, 163–64
Puchero, 107–8
Pudding
  Blood, Kid's, 102
  Bread, 160
  Southern, 161
  Easter, 165–66
  Walnut, 165
Pudin de Nogales, 165
Pudin Pascual, 166
Pumpkin Dessert, 158
Pumpkins, Drying of, 150
Pumpkin Seed Sauce, 133–34

Quail, Savory, 145–46
Quelites con Bacalao, 71–72

Rabbit, 137–39
  Cowboy-style, 138
  Sweet-Sour, 139
Rancher's Eggs, 59–61
  Border Style, 60–61
  Northern, 60
  Spanish, 61
Refritos con queso, 53
Rice
  Chicken with, 130–31
  Doves on a Golden Mesa, 140
  Fish with, 80–81
  Soup, Dry, 14
Roe, Indian, 69
Royal Duck, 147–48

Saffron, 13–14
Salads, xi–xii, 25–35
  Avocado and Grapefruit, 34
  Chilled Beet, 27–28
  Cold Cauliflower, 32–33
  Green, 28–29
  Green Bean, 30
  Green Chile, 27
  Potato, 29–30
  Shepherd's, 26
  Soused Chick-peas, 35
  Spring, 34–35
  Sweet Pepper, 31

Salsa de Chile Caribe, 38–39
Salsa de Chiles Frescas, 42–43
Salsa Colorada Oscura, 40
Salsa de Dos Chiles, 39–40
Salsa por Huevos en Torta, 65–66
Salsa Picante, 38
Salsa Picante Verde, 42
Salsa de Santa Fe, 41
Salsa Verde de Plaza, 43–44
Sangre de los Angeles, 5
Santa Cruz Chile & Spice Co., xiii
Santa Fe Chile Sauce, 41
Santa Fe Steak, 111
Sauces, 37–44
    Chile
        Coarse-ground Red (Number 2), 38–39
        Dark Red (Number 4), 40
        Fresh (Number 7), 42–43
        Hot (Number 1), 38
        Hot, Green (Number 6), 42
        Santa Fe (Number 5), 41
        Spanish Omelet, 65–66
        Two (Number 3), 39–40
        Country Green (Number 8), 43–44
    Hot, 38
    Hot, Green, 42
    Mole, 125–26
        Chicken in Green, 128–29
        Turkey in, 127
    Pumpkin Seed (Pipian), 133–34
    Spanish Omelet, 65–66
    Zucchini, Country Green, 43–44
Sausage. See Chorizo Sausage
Savory Beans, 53
Savory Lamb Chops, 109
Savory Pot, 117
Savory Quail, 145–46
Seafood. Sea also Fish
    Cocktails, 6–8
    Fish, 7–8
    Shrimp, 8
Shepherd's Chick-peas, 57–58
Shepherd's Salad, 26
Shrimp, 67–68
    Cocktail, 8

Fritters, 68
    from Nogales, 68–69
Sopa con Albondigas Agringadas, 22–23
Sopa de Chicharos, 18
Sopa de Garbanzos, 19
Sopa Seca de Arroz, 14
Sopa Seca de Tortillas, 15
Sopa de Tortilla, 24
Sopa de Verduras, 16–17
Soup, 11–24
    Broth with Custard Balls, 21–22
    Chick-pea, 19
    Clear Broth, 13
    Dawn Broth, 12
    Dry, 13–15
    Meatball, 22–23
    Pea, Unsplit, 18
    Rice, Dry, 14
    Tortilla, Dry, 15
    Tortilla, Wet, 24
    Tripe, with Hominy, 20–21
    Tripe, New Mexico Style, 20
    Vegetable, 16–17
Soused Chick-peas, 35
Southern Bread Pudding, 161
Southwestern Meatball Soup, 22–23
Spanish Hash, 113
Spanish Omelet Sauce, 65–66
Spareribs, 106
Spiced Pork Chops, 122
Spinach
    Salad, Green, 28–29
    Salt Cod, with, 71–72
Spring Salad, 34–35
Squash, 153–54
    Drying of, 150
    Sweet and Sour, 155
    Zucchini, Country Green Sauce, 43–44
Summer Squash, 153–54
    Sweet and Sour, 155
Sunfish, 76
Sweet and Hot Eggs, 62
Sweet-Sour Rabbit, 139
Sweet and Sour Squash, 155–56

Sweet Thingumabobs from Tubac,
  162–63

Tacos, 87–92
  Beef, 90
  Chicken, 88–90
  with Eggplant, 91–92
  with Marinated Pork, 90–91
  Picadillo for, 112–13
  Tacos con Berenjena, 91–92
  Tacos de Carne, 90
  Tacos de Gallina, 88–90
  Tacos de Puerco Adovado, 90–91
  Tamal en Cacerol, 97–98
  Tamale Pie, 97–98
  Tamales, 95–98
    Pork, 96
Tequila Cocktails, 4–5
Tomatoes, 149
Torrejas, 62–63
Torrejas de Camaron, 68
Torta de Carne, 116
Tortilla con Blancos, 66
Tortillas, xiii, 85
  Beans of Dawn with, 54
  Crisp Small, 9
  with Eggs, 66
  Flour, 85–86
    Burritos, 86–87
    Chimichangos, 87
    Chimichangos Dulces de Tubac,
      162–63
Tortillas de Harina, 85–86

Tortilla Soup
  Dry, 15
  Wet, 24
Tostados, 8–9, 87
Tripe, 19–20
  Kid's Blood Pudding with, 102
  Soup, New Mexico Style, 20
  Soup with Hominy, 20–21
Trout, 67
  Blue, 73
  Fried Mountain, 72–73
  Trucha Rellena, 73–74
  Truchas Azul, 73
  Truchas Montesas Fritas, 72–73
Turkey
  in Mole Sauce, 125–27
  Stuffed Roast, 132
  Tamale Pie with, 97–98
  Two Chile Sauce, 39–40

Veal, 117–20
  Cutlet, 118–19
  Stuffed Leg of, 119–20
Venado Bosque, 142–43
Vegetables, 149–55. See also spe-
  cific vegetables
Vegetable Soup, 16–17
Venison, 142–44
Victoria, La, 126

Walnut Pudding, 165

Zucchini Sauce, Country Green, 43–
  44